Kiss the Wind:

Understanding the
Elementals and Faeries

Victoria Hunt

OZARK
MOUNTAIN
PUBLISHING

For permission, serialization, condensation, adaptions, or for our catalog of other publications, write to Ozark Mountain Publishing, Inc., P.O. Box 754, Huntsville, AR 72740, ATTN: Permissions Department.

Library of Congress Cataloging-in-Publication Data

Hunt, Victoria, 1953

Kiss The Wind: Understanding the Elementals and Faeries, by Victoria Hunt

Understand the difference among elementals, faeries and elves and how these separate species impact the Earth in a way that is normally unseen to human eyes, but work together as a whole to keep our planet healthy and functioning smoothly.

1. Fairies 2. Elementals 3. Elves 4. Nature Spirits 5. Sylphs

I. Hunt, Victoria, 1953 II. Fairies III. Elementals IV. Title

Library of Congress Catalog Card Number: 2013947640

ISBN: 9781886940390

Cover Art and Layout: www.noir33.com
Book set in: Times New Roman, Californian FB
Book Design: Tab Pillar

Published by:

OZARK
MOUNTAIN
PUBLISHING

PO Box 754
Huntsville, AR 72740

WWW.OZARKMT.COM

Printed in the United States of America

DEDICATION

To the unseen forces upon whom we all depend

and to my loving family, here and departed.

May we always walk in truth and beauty.

TABLE OF CONTENTS

INTRODUCTION
The Elementals

Around the 16th century, a Swiss-German physician, alchemist, and magician named Phillippus Aureolus Paracelsus advanced an earlier alchemical theory that taught the concept that the primary elements of air, earth, fire, and water all consisted of subtle spiritual energies that animated each element in its natural state and was not to be confused with the physical matters of each. These spiritual energies, or Elemental spirits, partake in the nature of their own individual element and work within that structure to control the powers associated with its physical element. It's each of these Elements' spiritual counterparts that we'll strive to get to know better throughout the first section of this book.

Gnomes are the element Earth's spiritual counterparts, Sylphs are the element Air's spiritual counterparts, Salamanders are the element Fire's spiritual counterparts, and Undines are the element Water's spiritual counterparts. Medieval scholars knew the four elements as the "Four Winds," which were considered the original model sent forth by the One, the Source of all Being that brings life and substance to existence. In our modern day the four elements are still looked upon as the same visible and invisible elements our ancestors honored, for they are the building blocks that make up our world by giving it its substantial character and basic matter. They can also help us in manifesting any worthy goals we might be striving towards by lending their strength and power to these endeavors so that we can achieve our intended purpose.

Before we begin to work with the Elemental Kingdoms, we first have to understand the concept of the earth being not only physical but also spiritual in nature just as humans are not only physical manifestations but embodied spirit as well. Our organic human body is the "house" that surrounds our spiritual essence—that spark of divine energy we call us.

The energy systems that uphold humanity weave themselves within the same energy systems that move and control everything upon this earth, as well as the earth herself. It is Blessed Energy, Life-Force Energy, which is part of the ever-expanding mind of the *Creator*—by whatever name we choose to call it, for everything is of that Creation Source.

In fact, it is by this understanding we come to realize that humanity and the earth are one in spirit as well as one on the mundane physical level, for the same energy connects all things in creation. Thus, we can proceed to develop the idea of the Elemental Kingdoms of Earth, Air, Fire, and Water as the earthly elements infused with a spiritual awareness and resolve for maintaining animate, and seemingly inanimate, life on earth. They are the four fundamental qualities the ancient alchemists believed formed the world and contributed to all creation.

The four natural elements of Earth, Air, Fire, and Water can be at times both beneficial and destructive in their nature. For example, earth is the solid, material manifestation on the mundane level of physical existence. Earth is the foundation of the other three elements and the receptacle of all organic matter, for all is taken and birthed from earth as it gives structure to and sustains life. However, earth also takes back life, for it is where this manifested organic matter returns. When it has completed its time here, it unites with and greens the earth for other forthcoming forms of consciousness to receive substance and nourishment. Earth can also take life by force through earthquakes, landslides, and volcanoes, for such are the powers of earth, nature, and all the elements. They are fully what they are, neither wholly good nor wholly bad, just themselves in their own infinite manifestation.

The element of Air brings life-giving breath and pleasant scents. Through the winds, it blows in nourishing rains that fill our rivers and bring life to parched deserts, but winds can also blow in violent hurricanes and swirling tornadoes, thick blankets of blinding fog and ominous black clouds that send hailstones crashing onto earth to ruin crops and damage tender new shoots.

The Fire element warms us, cooks our food, and purifies. It can be seen as the Divine Spark of all existence, which manifests in and animates life, but fire can also absorb and destroy almost anything it comes in contact with. Fire is the hardest element to contain and can be very frightening and unpredictable.

The element of Water can cool and nourish, cleanse and heal. Humans and animals start life by being encased in amniotic fluid, floating and germinating in the great watery womb of their mothers, as all primordial life floated in the great salty sea of the Earth Mother. Water is second only to the element of air in being necessary for sustaining life.

Water is fluid and constantly changing whatever it contacts, for it shapes the land on which we live. This can be both helpful and harmful, for water can corrode, erode, and flood. Too much water and life drowns and molds; too little water, and life dries up and blows away. When learning to work with these elements and their spiritual counterparts, the Elementals, it's good to remember that knowledge and care is needed before commencing. Just like you wouldn't hop in an airplane and try to fly it before learning how the plane works and taking flight lessons, you shouldn't try to work with Elementals without understanding their power and how they operate—but that's one reason you bought this book, right?

Elemental spirits are one-element creatures. As such, they are unable to comprehend and assimilate life as we do. They are only capable of working within their own element, and this limits their evolution to a degree. By associating with multi-element humans, they can develop and evolve outside their specific levels of consciousness. This is one reason they consent to work with a human when that human shows concern and willingness to help them in this process. The Elementals work as a collective whole within each of their spheres to maintain the life of the planet and all that reside here, for that is their job as expert creators.

The world between humans and Elementals has always been close in proximity because humans are composed of the four elements of Earth, Air, Fire, and Water. Because of this, Elementals are much easier to contact than the nature spirits— better known as Faeries—for it's nearly impossible to determine where the Elemental world ends and ours begins. We are that intertwined.

Under normal circumstances you can't see, hear, touch, smell, or taste the Elementals. Because humans are visual creatures and need to *see* to make something real or believable, they'll use their imagination and natural visualization techniques that are inherent in them to work within the realm of Elemental energy by opening up to the Elemental's own environment and vibration. By doing so and trusting what comes to them, it is possible to work with the Elementals physically.

Before we explore the Elementals further, let's take a look at altars and casting circles since these concepts will be explored throughout this book, especially as I talk about the Elementals. Here is an overview to alleviate any possible confusion later.

Altars and Casting Circles

Casting a circle, also called creating sacred space, is the act of building a non-physical temple or sanctuary by focusing and expanding energy around you through the technique of creative visualization, which is rather like constructing a brick and mortar church using your mind instead of actual physical materials. You do this to establish a special holy place for a number of reasons: to celebrate the seasons, to empower one's self, to connect with Spirit, to set an environment for healing, to seek guidance and insight, to work magic, etc.

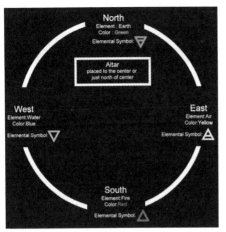

Inside your circle is the altar where your tools will be placed and your rite will be worked. These tools can include but are not limited to candles, incense and burner, matches, crystals, flowers, any personal preferences, and whatever your ritual requires. Ritual tools help you to focus on your intended purpose and are symbolic representations of certain aspects of magic, such as a bowl of water can represent the Goddess, the Elemental undines, healing, and the direction west. A small container of earth can represent grounding, Earth (the planet), Elemental Gnomes, fertility, birth, and the direction north while fire, such as the flame of a candle can represent, strength, power, the God, the Elemental Salamanders, and the direction south. Feathers, wind chimes, incense, smoke, the direction east, and the Elemental Sylphs can all be representative of the element air.

Any physical item will work for an altar. If your ritual is to take place indoors, a coffee table, dresser surface, shelf on a bookcase, TV tray, or even a cardboard box will serve whatever you feel is appropriate to your needs at the time. If you plan to work outdoors, a tree stump, flat stone, or cloth on the ground will work fine. Let your imagination guide you.

Some people keep an altar set up all the time, and others prefer one you can put up and down easily. If you have to transport your altar, it's much easier to have a lightweight one that you can carry.

The location to cast your circle and set up your altar is dictated by your personal preference, need, and weather conditions.

Some people prefer indoors while others choose to be outdoors in nature. No matter where you decide to hold your ritual, just make sure it's someplace you won't be disturbed. Remember to remain respectful to whatever area you've chosen, for you are then showing respect to Divine Source, that sacred flow of universal energy to which you are directly connected.

When your ritual is over, clean up after yourself. If you've used the natural outdoor world, remember to be respectful and protective. Put out any fires. Never leave trash around or mar nature in any way!

When casting a circle, you don't need to physically mark the ground, but some people desire to do so. Soil, salt, or stones are just a few of the choices used to define the space, which is normally nine feet in diameter but can be whatever size you might need, depending on the size of your work area.

Once you've set your intention for doing a ritual and have chosen the place to set up, the next step is to cast the circle. People have many ways to do this, but in the end it's what works for you. A circle can be cast by your visualizing a white or blue light defining the perimeter as you walk it, dance around it, sing it, or shake rattles. You can stand in the center and use your finger to trace it round or use a wand, sword, or knife. As I said before, it's all left up to how comfortable you are with what you're doing.

A circle is always cast by walking clockwise and taken down by the same method—only this time you visualize the energy flowing back to you and grounding down into earth.

After the circle is cast, calling of the Quarters is next. These Quarters are often named the Guardians by some or the Watchers by others and are considered to be the elements of Earth, Air, Fire and Water that the Gnomes, Sylphs, Salamanders, and Undines animate with life and substance. The Guardians are called to attend you at each direction (north, south, east and west). Usually you do this by starting in the east and going around, clockwise again, then ending facing east.

Next is performing the ritual. Some people would call this the "church service," but how you carry out this part will be in accordance with whatever your original goals may be and what you desire to accomplish.

After finishing your ritual, you then go about taking down your circle by going in reverse order of how you began: dismissing and thanking the Guardians for attending, walking the circle again, visualizing the energy coming back to you, and grounding it down into the earth. When this is done, put away anything you used that you don't want to leave out, and then go have a bite to eat. It's always wise to eat something after executing any ritual because that helps ground you back to the reality of the present moment. We wouldn't want you walking around in the *NetherLands* now, would we? That's not good for you or anyone else because accidents can happen that way!

Different spiritual traditions all have their own ways of creating sacred space, so if you follow a specific tradition, you can refer to their guidelines.

For more references to casting a circle and setting up an altar, I recommend *Pagan Ways* by Gwydion O'Hara, *Wicca: A Guide for the Solitary Practitioner* by Scott Cunningham, or *Celtic Traditions: Druids, Faeries and Wiccan Rituals* by Sirona Knight.

Now that you have a clearer understanding of altars and casting circles, let's return to the Elementals and meet the Gnomes, the first Elemental beings we'll explore. These are creatures of form who work hard in maintaining the physical structures of Earth, giving it color and a solid presence in our lives.

Kiss The Wind

CHAPTER 1
North: The Realm of the Gnomes

North is considered the direction of Earth and dwelling place of Ghob, the Gnome King, the guardian who lives deep within the land with the other earth Elementals and protects what is his. Gnomes are masters over all things associated with the earthly plane: trees, plants, animals, insects, rocks, minerals, and even our own human bodies, for we are all made from the organic matter of the element Earth.

When we desire to work with the Gnomes and all the Elementals, we must accept the fact that they exist and then get to know them. And how would you get to know a Gnome, you ask?

Gnomes are especially fond of rocks and stones, for rocks are the record keepers of all that has ever occurred through eons of time and dimensions of space in this universe. Rocks, crystals, minerals, and other earthly elements were all created within the same vibration of energy. By offering a rock or stone to Gnomes, you will give them the confidence they need to meet with you because they are related to those planetary substances and consider them to be family in a way; therefore, that encourages contact.

Rocks absorb negative energy, so by placing a rock on each side of the entryway into your home will assure that any negativity will be left at your front door and not be brought in by guests. Keeping an attractive bowl filled with pebbles on a table or counter-top will also balance out the energies inside your living space, for the Gnomes are the carriers of the sacred balance of earth and will add that balance to the inside of your house.

Finding a stone with a hole through it is considered especially lucky because not only is it a female emblem and representative of the Earth Goddess, but it's believed that by looking through a "holed" stone, one can see Faeries if the conditions are right.

Gnomes love nothing more than to delve deep within the earth searching for treasures like silver veins, crystals, and bits of lost or buried jewelry because they're miners who enjoy digging and tunneling into the dark crevices of the rocks and loam for such bits of accumulated finery. If you bury a coin or an unused piece of jewelry in a special place in your garden or out among nature somewhere, remember to say a prayer while you are burying it. Here's an example of one:

Ancient Gnomes, you who are of the Earth, I give this gift (of coin or gold or crystal, etc.) as an offering in peace and friendship between us and ask that you receive it in the light of the love in which it is given. May all be blessed because of our new and abiding friendship.

The Gnomes will take special notice of this. If it's accepted, you might see your garden start to increase in beauty and strength from that moment on because they've considered your offering worthy and have chosen to work with you by lending you a helping hand. Remember, you can't leave it all up to the Gnomes though, for you also need to share in the responsibility of caring for your garden and flower beds. The Gnomes will be most pleased as they love a good tilled garden almost as much as they love their rocks!

Composting is another way to get Gnomes to pay attention. Not only is composting good for the earth, but it's also beneficial to a garden, for compost feeds microorganisms that aids the plants and improves soil structure, which then helps the plant roots to penetrate it easier and makes a Gnome's job load lighter. Plus, the decomposing material of a compost pile is something no self-respecting Gnome could keep his hands out of, which is a win-win situation all around.

Gnomes reside over the season of winter when all has withdrawn into the earth to await rebirth in spring. This time of year allows us the opportunity to rest and reflect on all we've manifested through the comings and goings of the other three seasons, and the Elemental Gnomes will help here by keeping us grounded and burrowed down within the stability of earth. Winter can provide us a warm earthy hollow in which to manifest our hopes and dreams by keeping our thoughts turned inward as we gestate the new and dissolve the old. The Gnomes hold the energy for such regenerations. Asking for their assistance makes our journey more successful and grounded.

The astrological signs of the element of Earth are Taurus, Virgo, and Capricorn. Their psychological mode is sensate, perceiving by the physical senses of the body, which makes these three signs more frequently in tune with their five senses. They'll have a stronger affinity with Gnomes and be able to contact them more easily than the other signs since their predominate qualities are to be grounded, steadfast, disciplined, orderly, and sensual, which are all solid earthy attributes. Those born under the signs of Taurus, Virgo and Capricorn can be quite unmoving when they choose to be, but that only adds to their charm. They are anchors in a storm for their friends and family, someone people look to for stability when they, themselves, are lacking.

The physical needs of these three signs are generally of a higher priority than any of the other astrological signs, which is also decidedly earthy, for they, like the Gnomes, enjoy the tangible sides of life, solid matter that you can really connect with.

You'll find that Gnomes blend in quite well with the earthy outdoor colors because it's always extremely difficult to differentiate them from the landscape. They don't often appear in the surface world because they are very sensitive to extremes of cold and heat, so that is why they're generally only spotted in spring and autumn—if they are spotted at all. They much prefer their tepid underground environment where the extreme weather doesn't affect them.

 An equilateral triangle pointed downwards with a horizontal line drawn through the center of the triangle is the symbol of earth that's used by alchemists and magicians. This alchemical symbol indicates the earth's archetypal origins that are cold and dry and seek to descend, but its dry component blocks it as is indicated by the horizontal line drawn through it. Earth is the most fixed of the four elements, for it is of substance and form; however, for the Gnomes who create and color our world, it is an eternal artist's canvas, ever changing and evolving within its own carefully guided plan.

When calling on the assistance of a Gnome, paint the earth alchemy symbol onto a stone or piece of wood and place it in the north section of your altar or cast circle and say, "Hail and hearty be venerable Gnomes, you who bring grounding and stability and are the keepers of stones and bringers of the protective shield of earth energy, hear my call. I honor you." Then ask for their help in whatever your goals may be. Remember that it's the Gnome Kingdom that holds the power for the goals having to do with money, agriculture, fertility, construction, and aging, to name just a few.

Gnomes are the least volatile of the four elements and are the principle of the structure and material aspects of being, for Gnomes, like earth herself, are solid and weighty, balanced and centered, and can be relied to take care of that balance we all depend upon. Once you've established a relationship with a Gnome, you'll know that things will always be grounded right back to center one way or another because that is a Gnome's function and one of the things he seeks to contribute to the whole of existence.

Gnomes build their homes under aging trees, in abandoned wells and tunnels, caves, land masses, and cellars. They are said to have huge underground cities where they gather to work on the detailed handling of earth's needs. They are most interested in refining the solid weighty forms of earth and humanity into harmonious, blended energies that connect back to the Divine Source. By doing so, they help achieve a balanced and eternal stewardship of love and gratitude for the material plane of this universe, the plane that they so carefully guard.

The Nature of Gnomes

The Earth Elementals are those ancient miners and cave

dwellers who are older than time itself and care for nothing much other than digging underground and attending to the needs of the earth.

Gnomes come in various sizes like humans but are smaller in stature. Some cultures called them Dwarfs, Brownies, or Kobolds. If you get the chance to see them, they often look like wizen old men with bushy beards and parchment-like skin. They usually carry shovels and pickaxes, which they use to till the earth and wear earthy colors and close-fitting caps on their heads that are frequently deep red in color.

Gnomes are reclusive and avoid too much human contact. If you've ever caught a glimpse of something slipping behind a tree or disappearing into a hole in the ground, then you've experienced a Gnome sighting. They guard underground treasures, develop and maintain ore and mineral deposits, build (or destroy) mountains, and bring substance to organic matter for they know all the secrets of our manifest world. Being the closest Elemental to the vibratory rate of the earth, they are associated with gravity, ley lines, and the density of all things having to do with the physical plane.

Gnomes can be grumpy and hardheaded Elementals who refuse to work with humans that are untrustworthy or have offended them in any way. However, if they've grown to trust you and

5

are willing to work with you, then Gnomes can be friendly and jovial and will help you to manifest anything of a physical nature, like building a business, investing and making money, growing a garden, or moving up in your job or career.

Gnomes are gregarious by nature and usually like to work in small groups of their own kind; they believe there's strength in numbers, and strength is one of their virtues. They love to hide things and play tricks on unsuspecting humans. If you've ever come home from a hard day at work and laid your car keys in the usual spot only to find they're missing when you are looking for them later, then you've had yourself an encounter with a Gnome. Gnomes are never maliciously mean unless you've crossed them, so you'll eventually stumble across the mysterious vanishing keys sooner or later, either lying on the floor of your kitchen or on a shelf out in the garage where you parked your car. Just remember to say a quick thank you when you find them and try to appreciate the irritatingly good humor of a Gnome; if you do, chances are you'll always be a human the Gnomes look out for.

Gnomes like people who are grounded, level-headed, and diligent in their pursuits. They don't much care for the emotional types. They do enjoy a person who can make the most out of a bad situation—make lemons into lemonade, as it's said—and those whose eyes are turned towards taking care of the earth and fixing the damage humankind has inflicted on her. The Gnomes are the caretakers of this planet and by showing love and respect for the place we all call home, they'll be more willing to become involved with us. The Gnomes know that Earth is a sentient being that is ever changing, evolving, and self-regulating, and they will be more apt to share this understanding if you truly show that you care.

The Gnomes firmly know they aren't the *concept* of "being one with the earth," for they *are* the earth and ever aware of the changes and evolutions the earth experiences. They are the land, pressured and moving in an earthquake, they are the tiny pieces of shale that wear away and break loose from a mountainside, and they are the shifting white sands of a hot arid desert, moving back and forth sensually on top of a dune. They are the eyes and ears of this precious spinning orb in space that's called a planet, and they can open you up to see it all through their eyes, one grain at a time. Be aware and receptive, and the Gnomes will help you to achieve any worthy goal that is within their realm of solid earth.

The Winter Solstice

No matter how wet and cold you are, you are always warm and dry inside. Woodman's Adage

Since Gnomes hold sway over winter and the dark, we're going to examine the festival of the Winter Solstice or Yule, as the ancient Norse called it. In modern times, the Winter Solstice is generally celebrated on December 21st. The full moon of December is known as the Oak Moon or the Snow Moon. This is the dark time of year when the Earth Mother gives birth to the sun again, which is symbolized by the sacrificial death and rebirth of many an ancient deity: Horus, Dionysus, Mithras, Bel, and even Jesus. It is the longest night and shortest day of the year. It holds deep within itself the memory of death and rebirth, for after the night of the Winter Solstice, the sun seems to grow stronger, stretching out the light of day to the south until the Summer Solstice on June 21st when it starts to diminish again.

In the dark and dormant season of winter, we appear to reside in the womb of the Earth Mother upon whom we are all so dependent because inwardly we hold the vision of new life to be brought forth again in spring. For now though, we quietly rest and long for rebirth.

The Gnomes are busy in winter, for they start to energize the earth and prepare her for the spring activity. This is a good time to recognize and honor the Gnomes by filling your home with all the trimmings and greenery of the holiday season: holly and pine boughs, mistletoe and yule logs, ivy and pinecones, and even the great evergreen trees, like spruce, fir, and cedar. To not offend the Gnomes by cutting a tree just for the holidays and hindering all their hard work, it's best to buy a potted tree to celebrate. In honor of the Gnomes, in memory of the Winter Solstice, and as a new member of your family, you can plant the tree later in a nice spot in your yard where it will stand as a testimony to your willingness to work in a sustainable manner with the Elemental Gnomes to help keep the earth in balance. Find downed pine boughs and fallen mistletoe in the parks and forests near your home to ensure you harm no living thing. If you do need to cut a holly sprig or ivy stem, make sure you inform the plant of your intended action and reason first so it has a chance to prepare itself and release its spirit essence in the area you will cut. The Gnomes reside over all of the earthly aspects of our realm and assure its continuation. Thus, in gratitude for life recognized and taken, remember to either leave an offering of a pretty shiny bead or special stone for the Gnomes, a nut or seed for the animals, or a squirt of fertilizer for the plant as a token of thanks.

The yule log symbolizes the vegetation deity, the Green Man, who is associated with the plant kingdom. In the past the yule log was burnt, and its ashes were spread over the soil to help nourish and fertilize the earth. If you do burn a yule log— usually birch or oak—save a little of the ashes after the fire has gone out. Then place them in a bottle or jar, tie its neck with a red string or ribbon, and keep it in a south facing window of your house for protection of home and all who reside within— the Gnomes will ensure that it's done.

A wreath of grapevine, boxwood, or pine cones on your door or above the hearth is symbolic of the ever-circling round of eternity. It is the offshoot of the ancient solar cross, the cross within a circle that depicts the returning strength of the Divine Child—the Sun— in all its growing vitality and power.

Though Gnomes prefer the twilight hours over bright daytime, they honor the sun as one of the means needed to bring forth new life and growth; therefore, they'll acknowledge your effort in making a wreath and adorning it with the materials in their charge.

Ivy, pomegranate, oak, beets or most root vegetables, barley and wheat, tulip, wood sorrel, sage, quince, honeysuckle, and patchouli are other plants associated with earth and the Gnomes. For more references to herbs and flowers to entice Elementals, Scott Cunningham's *Encyclopedia of Magical Herbs* is full of useful information about the plant world and their magical uses. In addition, Nicholas Culpeper, an astrologer and physician of the early 17th Century, wrote *Culpeper's Complete Herbal*, which contains comprehensive descriptions of nearly all herbs and their medicinal properties for those who wish to create herbal remedies.

Gnomes delight in the groundedness of food and the bonds of family, so getting together with your friends and relations for celebrations is a very earthy activity which the Gnomes enjoy and will most likely participate in. Big meals, playful games, and brightly wrapped presents are a few things that delight Gnomes. Set a plate of food at one end of the dinner table overnight for the Gnomes, and in the morning dispose of it in your compost pile or bury it in the ground and know that the essence and energy from the meal has been taken in to revitalize the Earth Mother.

At this time of year in Britain, troops of costumed Morris dancers used to blackened their faces and sing while dancing through town. This celebration was to bring luck and to honor the night and the upcoming birth of the sun to ensure fertility and abundance for the earth. The Morris dancers still dance there today to wake up the earth with their sticks and bells to make sure an abundant harvest will be provided in the year to come. Gnomes were and are always well aware of the significance of this custom and participate in their own way, for they love the instrumental drums, beating in rhythm with the heartbeat of the earth—that pulsing life-force energy with its slow deliberate vibration.

If you desire to attract the attention of Gnomes, play music with drums or low-toned bass instruments. Better yet, learn to play a drum yourself. An Irish Bodhrán or a Native American hand-drum can be used to induce an altered state of consciousness in which we can become aware of other levels of energies and existence. When we want to work with them, we can attune to the inner fields and woodlands where the earth Elementals reside. Drumming will help you fine-tune and expand your powers of observation, helping stretch your vision to the subtle levels of the world of the Gnomes.

Gnomes and Your Garden

Start planning your spring garden after the night the winter solstice is over. You can take the left-over plants and flowers from your holiday decor, dry them, crush them, and then sprinkle them around the area where your garden will be placed in spring. As you do this, you might say something like this:

"Little Gnomes, as I sprinkle these herbs, may they light upon the ground as a tribute to the ever green and growing things of my garden, and may it prosper."

To entice the Gnomes so they'll know you're serious about forming a relationship with them, use rocks around your yard or garden. Make a rock fence or place a small stone circle in the center and it will help you connect to the Gnome's energy. Even by placing a small circle of standing stones in an empty flowerpot will appease them and draw them in.

Stone circles are natural meeting places for the Faeries and are said to take on a life of their own after dark. If you leave an offering at midnight on the night of a full moon—and the stars are lined up right—you might see them dancing in the center around a crystal throne where the Faery queen and king sit.

Gnomes love gardens, trees, flowers, and even lawns, for anything in place of concrete and asphalt helps restore the earth to her natural state and replenishes the underground water systems whenever it rains. The Undines also appreciate this. Flower gardens of natural indigenous plants not only bring joy to the beholder but also attract birds and provide food and shelter for their benefit. Birds are friendly with the Gnomes because they eat the bugs and worms that are part of the Gnome's earthly world. The bugs and worms hold no grudge against the birds, for everything has a natural order: one life gives away to help another survive. Air is also part of their realm, for they fly through the sky with the Elemental Sylphs and make their homes in the top of high reaching trees. When you get to know the creatures of the physical world, you begin the process of a relationship with the Elemental spirits and an abundant knowledge-filled life.

Personal Encounter with a Gnome

My encounter with a Gnome happened one spring day while I was walking in the woods by my house. Hiking down the winding pathway that edged the creek, I stopped to pick up trash. One soda can had inconveniently floated downstream and lodged against a fallen alder tree that stretched to the middle of the creek with the better part of its trunk still resting on the bank. Wondering how I'd ever get to it without getting wet, I stood and watched the can bob and shift with the current. Then I decided to chance precariously balancing myself on the tree trunk and walking over the water to the misplaced can, but first I moved to the opposite side of the trunk for better access. As I stepped over, I heard a voice.

"Hey! Watch where you're going!"

Looking down, I saw two feet sticking out of a hollow underneath the tree.

"Oh, excuse me. I'm sorry. I didn't see you there," I said rather surprised.

"Of course, you didn't. That's typical of humans. Do you always go clomping around in the forest like that without paying attention?"

Squinting against the early morning sun, he rose to his full four feet and growled, "Seems like an inconsiderate thing to do, seeing that you're so much bigger than most who reside here. Where you going anyway?"

I was feeling a bit embarrassed by my lack of attention, so I said in defense of myself, "Actually, I'm usually more aware of my surroundings, but I was sort of distracted by that can floating out there in the water," and I pointed to it.

"It's a pretty thing isn't it?" he said as he smiled at the can and softened a little. "Too bad it's nothing more than human rubbish. It's so shiny."

I turned my walking stick around and around in the dirt making tiny circles on top of each other and tried to avoid looking at him, for I was now embarrassed about that, too.

"Well, yes, that is unfortunate. And that was what I was focused on when I, um, stumbled upon you."

"I was watching the ants. That's what *I* was doing. Thanks for disturbing me," he said with a little *humph* after the last word. It sounded like it came from deep within the back of his throat and was meant as a dismissive pronouncement.

I wondered if I should apologize to him again but instead said, "I'll just go get it then and leave you alone so you can continue your observations."

As I started to step onto the tree, he said, "You know that tree trunk is going to be very slippery, don't you? It's wet, and if you try that, you're going to end up wetter than it is. Here, I'll get it." And he disappeared right in front of me.

Next thing I knew, the soda can went flying over the top of the bank and landed at my feet.

"There," I heard him say from nowhere. "Now you can get rid of it."

Wondering where he was, I glanced around and then noticed him sitting on top of the tree stump with his arms crossed over his chest. He eyed me suspiciously—like he doubted I'd really take the time to throw the can away.

I smiled. "That's pretty impressive. Can you disappear that fast anytime you want?"

"Humans! To you I disappeared. Really I was visible all along, but you don't think to look. You expect something entirely different, something supernatural, so that is what you'll get."

Now I was offended. He wasn't the first Elemental I'd seen before, but he was the first I'd seen disappear right in front of me, for they usually waited until I'd turned my head or blinked or something. Apparently, that was just a ruse to throw people off.

I bent over and picked up the can while he sat trying not to notice. Out of the corner of my eye, I could see him watching me, but when I'd look up, he'd quickly look away.

Finally he said, "You never answered my question. Where you going? Not that I really care, I just wanted to know because I've never seen you here before, and I wondered if you're one of those humans that can be trusted to care for the woodlands and forests. Those kinds of humans are pretty rare."

"What do you mean? You want to know if I can be trusted to take care of these places? Why couldn't you trust me? I've never done anything untrustworthy that could even be questioned."

I was irritated—and maybe a little defensive—because I wasn't used to having my character questioned. I'd prided myself on the fact that I tried in every way to be the kind of person that could be relied upon to do the right thing, especially when it had to do with nature because that was where my heart resided.

He took one big step back and said, "Now don't get huffy. I just see what your species does—the destruction and chaos that seem to come in the wake of your human living. How do I know you're any different from the rest? "

I'd heard this point before, so I replied, "Yes, I agree, humans are very destructive, but that doesn't mean we're all that way. I've been walking and working in this part of the forest for a long time, and there are others here who know and trust me. Besides, how do I know I can trust you, huh?" I knew that really wasn't an issue, but I wanted to defend my honor and stand up for myself.

With that said, I heard another "H*umph*" come out of him, and he disappeared again, leaving me feeling bewildered. Guess I had been a little hard on him, but fair was fair.

I walked over and dropped the can into the garbage barrel and thought, *He's right, of course; it is humans that trash the world and destroy nature, but not this human. I always pick up garbage, I recycle, and I never use pesticides in my yard. When I need to prune or remove any plants, I always let them know first so their spirit has a chance to move out of their body forms. I try to walk softly on the earth and be consciously aware. Once in a while I might err, but I try to always learn from it, so I can do better.*

As I walked along thinking, I heard a voice say, "Well, ok, maybe you aren't like all the rest, but that remains to be seen, doesn't it".

I turned and found him standing below a patch of bay trees with a hawthorn flower stuck behind his ear.

"Look," I said, "I think you owe me an apology. After all, if Elementals, and that includes you, weren't so darn judgmental, maybe some of us who are trying to do better and right the situation could feel happier in doing so. Nobody ever gets anywhere by crabbing and badgering someone. Trust me, I've had children. I know all about that," and I tried to stifle a smile at the memory.

With that said, I saw him start to smile and then chuckle, which made me start to laugh. It was infectious. He felt so different energetically when he was happy.

"Ok, you're right. I was heaping you in a lump with all the rest, but you have to see things from my point, too. We earth Elementals are the ones who keep the green and growing things doing just that. Without us the earth would be nothing but a barren wasteland unable to sustain any form of life as we know it. Plus it's our home that's being destroyed. How would you feel?"

"Yes, I totally understand where you're coming from," I agreed. "I know what has slowly happened over the last 400-500 years on this planet. The Divine Spirit dwelling in everything has been denied, and the world of nature has changed from being something you respected and honored for providing and maintaining life to something that needs to be beaten down and controlled. It's not a pretty picture, but I can't give up hope on humanity because I truly think we're becoming more aware of what we've done, and that's a step in the right direction. We didn't get to this point overnight, so getting back to holism won't happen that way either. Elementals need to be willing to work with humans to assist us in our quest for balance and understanding because in the life and evolution of humans, we're just about at the beginning of the toddler stage right now, so there's still evolving for us to do, and Elementals could help with that. Of course, there are many mature souls on this path, and I might be over-simplifying matters some, but you get the picture, right?"

"Yes, I get it. Of course, I do. Humans aren't as evolved as Elementals in this whole scenario," and he smiled mischievously.

I could tell he was kidding me, and maybe trying to get my goat again, and I knew he was right; we aren't as evolved. If

15

we were, we wouldn't be in our current situation. I smiled and thought to myself that in spite of his gruffness, he was actually starting to grow on me. I think he liked this banter going on between us, for it heightened the energy we were exchanging.

"So tell me," I said, smiling back at him. "Why haven't I ever seen you here before? What's your name anyway? Mine's Victoria."

He started hopping up and down in place and clapping his hands together, childlike.

"Pretty name. But you have to guess mine if you want to know it. I can't tell. You have to guess."

Was this going to be one of those 'You have to guess my name' from some Faery tale storybook? I wondered.

"Do we really have to do this? Couldn't you just tell me and save me the trouble?" I asked. "After all, I did tell you mine without you having to guess."

I knew that guessing his name would probably be impossible as he'd most likely never let it happen because then I'd be one up on him. Plus, Elementals consider names to be sacred, secret, and not to be shared except with only a choice few, for naming something brings it into being and applies a clear definition to it, which gives the other person control.

He smiled and said, "Now what fun would that be, huh? It's more exciting if you guess. Sooooo . . ." And he disappeared again behind a sycamore tree.

I yelled, "You didn't say hide-and-go-seek. You said guess your name. Don't I even get a clue?" I was looking all around for him to reappear—overhead in the tree branches, down the path in front of me, over the edge of the creek bank.

"Come on. Not fair! Give me a clue."

"I just did," I heard him say behind me, which made me jump.

16

I whirled around and caught him about ready to throw flower petals in my hair just to be funny.

"Hey, stop that," I laughed. "Is that supposed to be some sort of clue or something? Flower petals. Your name's Flower?" I saw him scowl and then laugh, "Ha. That would be too easy, so try again."

Now it was my turn to tease him. "How about petal? That's it! Petal!" He decidedly did NOT look like a Petal, but I was poking fun at him.

"Very funny. Try again."

"Well, let's see," I said. It looked like I really was resigned to guessing.

"You disappeared behind a sycamore tree. You were standing underneath bay trees. You wear green . . . You're ornery. Does that count?" And I laughed at my own jab at him. "I don't know. I'm not very good at guessing games. Never was."

I got another guttural "Humph," and he was gone again.

Sure gets upset easy, I thought rather annoyed, so I turned and headed for home.

When I got back to my house, I went into the backyard to do some cleanup work. I needed to rake what was left of the leaves and get them piled up by the side of the road because the city's Leaf Pick Up Program was ending soon, and I wanted them to go off to the green-waste recycling. The once colorful leaves of fall had dried and turned brown as they were blown and tossed around in the yard by the winter winds. As spring approached, what was left of them had pushed up against the edges of the fence and hidden underneath the birdbath and decorative rock of my landscaping, so they had to be hand-picked out of the corners because I didn't use a leaf blower, for I found them way too loud for my sensibilities, and I consider it noise pollution to the max!

17

While down on my hands and knees with my head cocked to one side as I tried to see beneath the ivy, I heard the clearing of someone's throat as if the person was trying to get my attention.

"Huhhhh . . . huhhhh."

I knew it was him but decided two could play this game, so I conveniently ignored him.

After a minute or two, he said, "I know you know I'm here, so it won't do any good to continue feigning ignorance." And I could tell he chuckled in spite of himself.

Determined not to let him have the upper hand, I then looked up. This was turning into a battle of wills.

"I don't have time for this, you know. Either you stick around, or you don't—your choice."

His face lit up like someone had just turned on a light bulb. Then he said, "You mean around here in your garden? Well, madam, I'd be delighted to. It would be lovely to take up residence here. Thanks." And he bowed low. "But just because I'm moving in, don't get you off the hook for guessing my name. You let me know when you get it, ok?" And with that he wiggled his index finger at me, then stuck it in the air and vanished.

The Rest of the Story

The gnome did move into my garden in the backyard, and he's made quite a difference. Everything I plant there grows better and faster than it used to. I had dug up a sprouted acorn from the land where my tree friend King Oak had grown before he was tragically cut down and then planted it in my backyard in remembrance of him. Unfortunately, it had accidentally been cut off two or three times by people mowing my lawn in the previous years. Poor thing! I eventually placed a stake alongside it so the mowers would remember to be careful and not continue to cut it off. After my Elemental friend moved in, it started growing like crazy.

My dad finally said to me one day, "What's up with that oak tree? I've never seen one grow so fast; usually they're slow growers. Sure must like it here."

The grapes on my grapevine are twice the size they used to be, and my lemon tree gives off huge apple-sized lemons. Thanks to my Elemental friend, for years now I've had the most marvelous display of purple morning glories on my fence, and all the other plants are as happy and abundant as can be. I'm grateful for his tender loving outdoor care.

Sometimes he'll wander into the house and leave me an earthworm or two in my family room as a gift, but mostly he cares for my garden. We've learned to get along tolerably well, but even after all these years, I still haven't figured out his name. Maybe one day he'll just break down and tell me, but I'm not going to hold my breath for that one.

Kiss The Wind

.

CHAPTER 2
East: The Realm of the Sylphs

The next Elementals we'll look at will be the Sylphs, those beings of the air whose queen is Paralda. Sylphs are linked to the mind and the east, the direction of illumination and manifestations. Though the Sylphs, like the other three Elementals, are assigned to a particular direction, each Elemental spirit is everywhere within its own element and not confined to one specific location on a map.

Rebirth, renewal, and the flow of knowledge and wisdom are also qualities of the east, which is where we look to when dealing with other goals like change, movement, intuition, learning, creating, and communicating. It's here that we search for clarity of mind and spiritual awakening, for the Sylphs were at the beginning of creation and govern clear thinking. If you want to create anything new in your life: be more organized; speak in public; take a trip out of town; write a book, poem, or article; return to school, etc., call upon the Sylphs to help achieve these goals.

Although I am a Pisces and a water sign by birth, my primary psychological mode is thinking, which comes naturally to me and is represented by the element Air. I employ thought greatly in everything I do—in fact, sometimes even to my own detriment. I find that if I don't curb this tendency, I tend to over-analyze everything until I analyze myself into a position of not being able to make a decision—an obvious sign that the other three elements of my personality need to be more developed. For me, Air is a no-brainer (figuratively speaking), Earth is strong on my temperament scale, but Fire and Water, which are almost equal, are somewhat less in relation to this scale. To find your own strong and weak modes, take the test found in David Kiersey and Marilyn Bates book, *Please Understand Me.* Why? If the primary goal of the evolving spiritually minded person is to understand what areas need to be balanced and worked on, then finding out your temperament modes will help.

The three astrological signs of Air are Gemini, Libra, and Aquarius. These signs are generally adaptable, spontaneous, and energetic. They are often more extroverted than most other signs and have a cloaked innocence that is truly endearing—if they ever let you find it! Air signs have a stronger association with the psychological mode of thought.

The predominate qualities of Gemini, Libra, and Aquarius are intelligence, quick wittedness, versatility, and independence, plus an extremely great capacity to multi-task, which is an ability we wish we all had. Their gift of connecting with the Sylphs almost instantaneously is the stuff of legends, for the Sylphs embody all the qualities these three signs hold and lend to them their strengths and insights in moving along their chosen life paths.

These three Air signs have an innate desire for knowledge and enlightenment, which emerges at some point in their lives, sparking them to seek deeper wisdom of the universe. Many other signs choose to ignore this awakening unless their primary temperament mode is thinking. Gemini, Libra and Aquarius use the energies of the mind with the strength of the wind to create beauty and transmit knowledge from the Divine to humanity, for they come closer to knowing the element of Air—the very Sylphs themselves.

After my book, *Animal Omens* was published in 2008, I found it difficult to get any inspiration flowing for another book. I was trying hard to produce something I felt of worth, but it just wasn't happening. I'd heard about writer's block, but I felt that I had writer's dam instead. I knew something was there roaming around in the back of my head, but I couldn't quite latch onto it. The more I tried, the worse it got until I figured I was going to be one of those "one-hit-wonders" and gave up.

Then in March of 2010, I was laid up with pneumonia, felling crummy and sorry for myself. On one particular day I went outside to sit in the sun and get a little Vitamin D. It was a perfect day for the Sylphs to come calling because the day was warm with a beautiful blue sky, white wispy clouds, and a slight breeze. When I relaxed back in the chair and closed my eyes, they did. Suddenly appearing behind my closed eyelids were multitudes of little colored sparkles dancing around and gesturing at me to follow them. I wasn't sure what this meant but felt inspired to run inside and get paper and pen. I sat down and started to write this story:

The Creation Story

Before there was anything, there was the Void. And in the Void dwelt the One of Many Names, circling itself in this dark field of space, content with the infinite cycle of being.

Over what humankind now calls time, the One of Many Names longed for something other than its own knowing and enlightenment; it desired to penetrate the Void with something other than itself. So the One sang a single tone from its center and sent it spiraling in and out of awareness. It rested in the darkness of the Void and waited to be heard in the infinite realm of space.

As this tone gestated, surrounded by the protoplasm of the creative force, it grew and burned, sending the spark of Divine Knowledge it had received from the One out to create more Spirit amongst the dark fields of space. The One was glad, for it perceived what it had created.

Slowly, this Spark of Spirit cycled, building strength and power gradually over eons of infinite space and time until it released itself in a single burst, like an orgasm, and sent the abundant life force from the One into its own center, creating more diversity amongst itself. Time came and went. This diversity developed and separated into many who added their own tones, sending beautiful music forth into the infinite— music which no human words can now describe, for it was music of Divine Love and Union.

And so all that ever was, is, or will be was created first by tone in Spirit before it was housed in organic matter, and these Spirits in all their diversity dwelt in the vast and great sea of being, and they were one with it in joy.

The Inspirational Sylphs

On that special day, I opened, and the Sylphs arrived, bringing the inspiration I had been seeking. A few days later, the dam broke and the floodgates were torn down as I sat in bed and began this book, which was directed by the inspirational Sylphs who are said to gather around artists and poets to assist in the process of creating. Like my first book, this inspiration flowed with urgency down through my crown chakra and into my fingers without me having to do much thinking about it, which was perfect since I didn't have time to over analyze and possibly squelch it. It moved like the very Sylphs themselves, beautifully fluid and graceful, which was a testament to me that they can help us achieve great things if we'll just let their breezy gifts of inspiration blow us in the right direction like they did for me and can do for anyone.

The Nature of Sylphs

The Sylphs have no specific physical form. They are very ethereal and can appear as humans. When they do take on human form, they generally are very tall and beautiful with long thin arms and legs, angular faces, and somewhat transparent bodies. They are lively, friendly, changeable, and somewhat eccentric. Being creatures of the air, they make excellent messengers, getting information and thoughts from one place to another in a matter of seconds.

The axiom "Energy follows thought" is true, so being careful of what one thinks is good advice, for negative thoughts only add to the discord that you'll so often find in the world today. This negative energy and thought process permeates all densities and elements of our universe and eventually travels back to us, producing a domino effect in our lives. Thoughts are indiscernible like the wind, so to have an unkind thought or feeling about something or someone can produce that negative energy coming back to you before you realize it, which doesn't mean we should walk around ignoring how we feel and giggling all the time, but it does mean that we need to be aware of those aspects that are causing our stresses and grief and learn to work with them in a correct and positive manner to alleviate any negativity that might be causing us harm.

If you want to have healthy communications with people and improve your relationships, the Sylphs can help stimulate that. Healthy communication means to truly hear and understand what the other person is saying and feeling, so asking a Sylph to join you when having a serious conversation with someone is a wise thing to do, especially if you want to resolve any issues and strengthen your relationships. Their power in making communication flow naturally between people is a great gift, which they'll share when asked.

Sylphs are the first to be invoked in ritual and magic because they are associated with the east which is the direction of spiritual knowledge, hidden secrets, and the place where old gods are believed to dwell. Also, the Sylphs move the energy of a magical working by increasing the vibration to a higher level and thus opening a portal into other dimensions. The Sylphs have access to our earthly libraries, as well as other forms of esoteric information and records kept in the different realms of time and space which are not readily seen with the human eye, like the Akashic Records.

Incense is generally used when doing ritual work because it helps contribute to the potency of the atmosphere. Sylphs like scents and enjoy playing in the smoke the incense produces, so they'll gather inside your sacred space to inspire and give expediency to the prayers and workings of the rite you're conducting by carrying them upward to the Higher Mind or Source where our goals and desires are manifested.

Sylphs also enjoy music. Sound travels through air, so having music in your home will encourage the Sylphs to join you there. They're particularly fond of wind instruments like pipes, flutes, and harmonicas and also enjoy a beautiful song. They'll even respond to whistling if you're good at it.

The Sylphs like to travel on the breeze and play in the clouds. If you've ever felt your hair ruffle or something softly touch your face when no one was around, then you can count on the fact that it was a Sylph trying to get your attention. Were you listening?

Sylphs love hot air balloons, motorcycles, planes, speed boats, hang gliders, and parachutes—all those things that involve speed, wind, air, and movement. They are said to live on mountaintops and delight in flying with the winged creatures, especially eagles. When you find yourself outside on a clear sunny day enjoying the landscape, look for those tiny glistening sparkles dancing around in the air. If you see any, you'll know you've been lucky enough to witness Sylph activity and the door between the worlds opening. Not only do the Sylphs dance in the wind, but they can also pull back the veil to the Otherworld—home of the Gods, Faeries, and Ancestors—affording humans the opportunity to get in touch with those who reside there. The colors of the east, yellow and white, are associated with the Sylphs. These are also colors of the sun and the wind and embody the qualities of self-development, change, and independent thought. White is also the color of divinity, purity, and transcending to a higher vibration. Yellow is a color of happiness, joy, the mind, and a positive attitude toward life that we can use to help make our life path less stressful and base, for all colors are associated with a specific vibrational frequency that can be used in healing.

The alchemical symbol of air is an equilateral triangle pointed upward towards the sky with a horizontal line drawn through  the center of the triangle. Air is hot and moist, so it is caught between two extremes of the realms above and below, which are thus symbolized by this line running through the triangle. Air is suspended between time and space where intuition lives, so the Sylphs are the beings that provide us access to this inspired intuition because air is the medium that facilitates the travel of all invisible forces.

When you desire to work with the Sylphs, you can draw the alchemical symbol of air with a feather as you face east. Stand before your altar or inside the circle you have cast and say:

Element of Air, Old Ones of the East, you who witness the birth of the sun each day and bring us movement through change, add your power, Eastern Friends, and help me to drink from your cup of inspired wisdom. Blessed be.

The Sylphs will pick up your prayer on the wind and see that it is heard by the powers that help manifest our dreams and desires.

Our sense of smell is also associated with the Sylphs, for scent is carried to our nose through the very air we breathe. Breath is very important when meditating and "journeying." To reach the altered states of consciousness used to travel to the different levels of awareness requires breathing in a correct manner called the "cleansing breath." By watching a baby sleep and breathe, you can learn how to do this by taking similar breaths from deep inside your solar plexus/third chakra and then moving them up and outward through your mouth like babies do. Visualizing each breath as a drawing in of white or gold light and then slowly breathing out a black mist of negativity will help your body release any tensions associated with stress and stagnant energy because every time you take a breath of air, you are restored to your authentic self through the energy-bridge that connects your mind and body. Most humans breathe too shallow or forget to breathe at all for a time, so practicing the "cleansing breath" will help clear the way for a more healthy life and assist the Sylphs in sharpening our intellect and creativity.

The Spring Equinox

The Wind does not keep secrets well. V.H.

March 21st is the set date of the Spring Equinox. It's the time of year when the flowers start to bloom, trees leaf out, and the earth greens. The light is still slowly increasing as it casts aside its dark mantle of winter to give way to the bright new sun being birthed.

In medieval England the full moon was called the "chaste moon," but in the Celtic countries the full moon was known for what it truly is, Moon of Winds. It's this time of year when the Sylphs can be most unpredictable—and annoying. The winds of March are ever testing us, bringing in torrents of rain and bad weather one day, only to reveal beautiful blue skies and gentle breezes the next.

If March comes in like a lion, it will go out like a lamb; however, March is a changeable month, so it could turn the other way around. This well-known saying actually comes from astrology. When the constellation of Leo (the lion) rises higher in the eastern sky—the direction of the Sylphs—Aries the ram (representing the lamb) gets lower in the western sky.

The clear warm days of spring brings wispy white clouds slowly moving across an electric blue sky. The white transparent images of angels emanate from these cloud formations, attesting to the domain of the Sylphs, for they are elements of air who enjoy the wide open space of the sky and will often appear as cloud beings. This is an excellent time of year to hang wind chimes on your porch or in a tree. As the breeze blows the chimes, the soft sound of tinkling glass or ringing metal will bring the Sylphs closer, for they are enchanted by music in its many forms, and it's they who animate the wind and play in it, opening the way for the chimes to sing their sweet melodies.

Sylphs love flowers, especially honeysuckle, lavender, gardenia, rose and sweet pea. To attract the attention of Sylphs, place dried rose petals or honeysuckle flowers—any other nicely scented flower will do as well—on a charcoal block facing east, light it and wait for the smoke to waft up into the sky. As it catches and flies higher, say this:

Beautiful Sylphs, bringers of fresh air, new perspectives and awakenings, look down from your high thrones and accept my offering. Help me to play, to dance, to sing, and to breathe deeply your life-giving air. Acknowledge my presence and help me walk my path in strength wherever the winds might take me. Thank you.

The Sylphs will catch the scent floating in the air, absorb it, and move in close to you. As you go throughout your day, you'll notice a sweet flowery scent occasionally lingering around you. That will be the Sylphs thanking you for taking the time to please them, which is a step in the right direction if you're trying to establish a relationship with them.

The aspen tree is also a part of nature that's associated with the air element. The rustling whisper of wind through aspen leaves testifies to the joy of the Sylphs in play as they careen through the branches of this beautiful white wood tree. The aspen's physical link is to family groups, immortality, speech and language while its spiritual aspects are linked to the protection and shielding of the deity Mercury, the god associated with air.

The Christian world celebrates Easter in March, but for the old pagan religion, March was the time of year to honor the earth in her guise as the goddess of birth and rebirth. The word Easter is a derivative of "Eoestre," the name of an Anglo-Saxon fertility goddess who released the plant life from her dark winter womb to bring fresh renewal in spring and another year's growing season. She is believed to take the form of a white rabbit—the rabbit being symbolic of fertility—and makes her way around the world bringing new life and abundance to the land and, in turn, to the community members. The Goddess Eoestre assures us protection on our journey through the dark realm of death, for she is Goddess of the East, the Lady who gives the blessings of a new life and a new beginning when all has been silent through the long cold of winter.

People of the old religion gave colored eggs as offerings in spring to the Goddess Eoestre. They placed these eggs, symbolizing fertility and birth, on graves to ensure the rebirth of their ancestors and to honor their bloodline.

Celtic druids were said to use an egg-shaped object—possibly made from glass or shells—as a talisman for resolving certain legal disputes, focusing and regenerating the Self on the inner plane, and directing life-force energy associated with rebirth. As spiritual leaders, lawmakers, and counselors, the druids used a treasured egg-shaped object called an "adder stone" because it held many magical properties only they could access. In Scotland's woods, heaths, cliffs, and mountains, the adder lives. The adder, called "nathair" in Gaelic, is a poisonous snake though its bite is rarely deadly. To the Earth Goddess and the Sun God, this snake is one of their central totem animals. The Welsh bards in the ancient druid tradition used to call the druids "naddreds" or "adders," and it was this snake that the adder stone symbolized. The snake was a fertility symbol and represented the creative and regenerative power of the universe and humanity's connection to that power.

In springtime the Sylphs fly softly through the air, bringing us fresh cleansing breaths, freedom of movement in this space we call a planet, and messages of hope, which can merge us with the Source. So raise your hand to the sky, blow a kiss to the wind, and say a prayer of thanks for this newly found knowledge and freedom. Then soar!

My Freedom in Flight Experience

My own freedom in flight happened spontaneously while I was seeking the answer to an ache and longing in my heart. It was my first real glimpse into the world of the Sylphs.

A bright glimmer of light weaved slowly through the trees, growing closer as I reached for it, heart pounding, only to see it slip through my fingers and dissolve unhindered into the ground at my feet.

I'd walked into the forest searching for a way to quiet the longing in my heart, a feeling I could no longer ignore by pretending it didn't exist. Now that I was there, though, I wondered where my guidance might come from?

I leaned against a tree and felt its energy root me to the ground as the tree was rooted. The sun had just risen over the tree canopy and pooled warmly on my left. Then it lingered and started to shift away as I watched its light surround each leaf and stem of plant. While it moved on, I saw what remained was not the aftereffects of the sun, but the aura of each living plant and tree, glowing with a life-force as brilliant as a cut diamond.

As I waited with eyes closed, I spread my arms in reverence and suddenly felt totally in tune with Spirit and the subtle dance of the unseen. I held my breath, lest I disturb the growing magic, and realized that I was now out of body and off like a feather in the wind. My spirit was carried along on the current of a breeze while my body still rested upon the earth.

Higher and higher I flew, up past the scented pines and the hawks riding the wind, up where the spirits of air frolic and play. I was no longer me but a higher vibration—me in my true state of pure energy, resonating with the Source and set adrift in the endless flow of the Sylphs as they moved me along, laughing and free.

Up ahead I faltered, for something tugged the silver thread at my solar plexus that attached me to my earthbound body. I knew I had flown far enough, for in my joy I'd gone adrift in this lucidness with which I'd joined.

Unexpectedly, I became dizzy and started to fall when a soft but clear humming caught me and seemed to buoy me up like I was cushioned on a fluffy white cloud. Then again I saw the Sylphs, shimmering and luminous, stirring ghostly in the void around me like waves lifted higher with the force of wind, savoring the feel of weightlessness and vibrating along the boundaries of our two worlds of form and formlessness. They spilled out into the air. No, they *were* the air, aligning with the flow of the Otherworld, with Source—so happy, so blessed.

I inhaled, and they shattered apart, whirled, floated, and were gone from my sight. My head was aching as I opened my eyes to find I was back in my body with my open hands at my side, turning slowly back and forth as if I was still in flight, but no, I was back.

It was then I knew that the longing I'd felt was from a desire to belong again, as I once had, to the immense creative Source, to feel a part of something bigger than the life I lived.

Now I try to put into words the connection I felt that day when I let myself be still long enough to melt like ice into formlessness, drawing back the curtain long enough for those who flew with me to say, "Fear not, for you are safe even when reaching beyond the veil to touch the planes of the Otherworld. Welcome, fellow traveler."

Kiss The Wind

CHAPTER 3
South: Realm of the Salamanders

In the direction of the south lie the fiery Salamanders. Here Djinn is the awesome ruler. The colors most associated with the Elemental Salamanders are red, yellow, and orange, but white, blue, and green can also be seen in the flames of fire they animate, so these colors also have a place in their realm.

The alchemical symbol for fire is an equilateral triangle pointed upwards. Fire is hot and dry and seeks to ascend and shift, which represents change through what some call the  "refiner's fire" or "kundalini rising." Kundalini is an electromagnetic force that lies at the base of the spine in the root chakra of humans. When it rises up the spine naturally—usually around mid-life—it enables us to become more spiritual, holistic beings by bringing purification in the form of transcending our baser selves to connect directly to the Source. Kundalini is that spark of life-force and power that the Salamanders stimulate throughout our bodies and is a major agent of change, like fire itself.

When you wish to call forth the Salamanders in a magical working, face south and lift your voice high while making the alchemical symbol for fire with a lit candle. Then say:

"As the white heat of the fire burns within my heart, so shall it bring light out of darkness. Honorable Salamanders, lend your presence to my sacred space with passion and strength. You are recognized now and always. Please join me."

Then know that they are present and ready to assist you in manifesting your desires.

When people think of the South—at least those who reside in the Northern Hemisphere—they might think of sand, heat, and sun, but on a more primal level south is the direction of the power of masculine energy. The Salamanders rule the basic manifestations of these energies, which are purification, will, virility, and passion—in other words, that which gives the intensity with which they are synonymous.

The sun is the principle source of heat we here on planet earth rely on for survival. Strength of will is also associated with the sun, which our ancient ancestors worshiped and honored because the sun was considered a gift from the gods. Since humans were first given fire to keep them warm, cook their food, purify against disease and infection, and light the darkness of the night, fire has been known as one of the most essential and powerful elements on the planet. Fire is literally bound to no one because it has a will of its own. Fire can consume air, but the lack of air can also squelch a fire, for fire needs air to survive. Without the spiritual Elemental Salamanders, not a fire in the entire world would be possible because it is they who animate physical fire.

When you wish to be successful in competitions/contests or gain and maintain good health, face south and work with the Salamanders to manifest these goals or other fiery goals, like protection, sexual prowess, loyalty, and courage. Salamanders have a tendency for over-kill because of their excitable nature, so the first rule of thumb is to make certain your relationship with a Salamander is built on a strong, solid foundation before you proceed. You can then go ahead with sufficient confidence in attaining your goal once you have a firm grasp on the fundamentals of the element of fire.

Three astrological signs are attributed to the element of fire, which are the signs of Aries, Leo, and Sagittarius. Fire-sign people can be impulsive, short tempered, and self-absorbed, but they can also be warm, gentle, self-confident, and very intuitive. If they tell you not to purchase that home overlooking one of the Great Lakes, you'd better think twice before signing the final papers.

These three signs are natural leaders, even if sometimes this quality doesn't show up until later in life. They are loyal to friends and family, but don't cross them because they can easily lash out at the unsuspecting with great speed and a sharp bite. It truly hurts when you've been "bitten" by a fire sign. Remember that the Elemental Salamanders are known for their volatile nature, so you've been warned.

Aries, Leo, and Sagittarius are independent and would rather do things themselves. That way they are assured to get all the glory and attention they feel they rightfully deserve, but don't get too upset with them. In the end they were the ones that put all the time, effort, and heart into the project; and heart is something we all need a little extra of, so just look to an Aries, Leo, or Sagittarius for that special warm, personal touch. Then all that jealousy and aggravation you have for their incredible ability to get things accomplished will miraculously melt away.

The psychological mode of Aries, Leo, and Sagittarius as fire signs is intuition, for this is their innate ability, their "inner fire" so to speak. This delicate awareness helps them define their lives and over time teaches them to trust themselves and their understanding of the world in which they live. Learning to honor that is one of the great challenges they must face. The other challenge is learning how to share power—in other words, letting go of control. The control issues in a fire sign's life have to do with their independence and their utter need to be self-governing. You'll never find them taking the back seat to anyone if it's at all possible, but that just comes from the same temperament found in the fiery, aggressive, in-control Salamanders. We all need good, solid leaders in our lives who have mastered themselves and can lead with a true heart, and a balanced fire sign can achieve this.

If you truly want to learn to work with the Salamanders, it would be wise to get to know a few Aries, Leos and Sagittariuses first. Then you'll be well on your way.

The Nature of Salamanders

The spirited salamander is the most difficult of the four Elementals to describe, for when they do manifest into form, it is usually as a lizard-like creature crawling in the middle of a blazing fire, but they are so fast in their movements that to actually catch a glimpse of one is pretty rare. They like to readily change forms to confuse those who are trying to invoke them—it takes a centered and well-balanced individual to keep control of a Salamander—so it's best to master working with the other three Elementals first before you attempt any contact with a Salamander.

Paracelsus noted that a salamander can take the appearance of balls of fiery red-orange light running across fields and meadows and floating over water at night. They are said to animate a phenomenon called St. Elmo's Fire, which is a type of continuous electrical spark associated with tall pointed objects like church steeples and ships' masts and are seen when the air and ground below a storm becomes electrically charged.

Salamanders transmit the energy/divine spark of life from the Higher Realm that charges the electrical impulses that make the human mind, nervous system, and heart function. People with explosive tempers, control issues, and a desire to dominate have an overabundance of the fiery salamander nature in their psychological mode, which is one reason to make sure you are in a state of balance before contacting them. It's easier for these imbalances to get out of hand and become a problem when you're not psychologically healthy. Salamanders are explosive by nature, so they can imprint this same temperament onto an already unhealthy mental state, which will cause unnecessary stress and strain.

After you've established a relationship with them, Salamanders can be very loyal. They can also be very hypnotic. Have you ever sat staring into the sinuous leap of flames that animate a campfire at night and gotten lost in it? That is the salamander at work, for fire is one of the elements that can mark a portal into the realm where different lifeforms reside, like the ancient primordial gods, the Faery beings who work within nature, and our honored dead—the ancestors. So unless you have the upper hand with a Salamander, it's best to be extra careful not to fall under their spell—an easy thing to do in light of their ability to take us where we might not yet be ready to go.

When working with Salamanders, remember to always clearly define the boundaries between you and them. Do not allow them to push beyond these boundaries, for they will certainly try. They are strong-willed and used to having their own way. Learning how to draw the line with a salamander is paramount in ritual work because they are not easy to control with their excitable temperaments. When your relationship is sound and they understand how you will work together, they'll be more willing to conform to the rules you've set down. Then you can press forward with trust and assurance.

The legendary phoenix is a mythical representation of the element of fire. The ancient Greeks, Egyptians, and Assyrians

Phoenix Bird Stencil
www.spraypaintstencils.com

associated this bird's fiery death and rebirth with the cycles of the sun, which dies every night and is born again each morning. The Egyptian story of the phoenix tells that it lives five hundred years. When it senses its emanate death, it creates a nest of cinnamon, spikenard, and myrrh in the top of a date palm and sets the nest on fire to be consumed along with it. Once it is burnt to ashes, a new phoenix emerges to live and grow until it is strong enough to carry its nest from the tree to the Egyptian city of Heliopolis where it placed it in the temple of the sun. Then the phoenix starts its life-cycle again. The triumph of the phoenix over death by fire is symbolic of the properties of the fire element. It is the active agent of change for helping ignite the spark of life at the very core of being, which the Elemental Salamanders transmute into existence in our physical reality.

A ceremony to work with the Salamanders is to sprinkle herbs associated with fire, such as bloodroot, hawthorn, frankincense, cinnamon, nettle, and/or palm into a candle flame or bonfire as an offering to the Salamanders while you visualize the herbs being consumed and your prayers being heard. Say a word or two about their undying courage or their ability to purify, and your offering will carry more weight in getting their attention next time you desire their assistance. They can be a bit vain at times, and it never hurts to appeal to this side of them—in all sincerity, of course.

On a more emotional level, Salamanders respond to acts of courage, displays of strength of character, or passion in any undertaking, including lovemaking. The Elemental Salamander is not shy when it comes to well-placed passion, so neither should you be. Next time any of these three comes up, invite a Salamander to join you. You might find you're glad you did, for you could discover a little something extra added to your undertakings.

The Summer Solstice

To be a guardian of the scared flame, you have to dance with it and use that energy to fuel your magic. VH

The Summer Solstice, or Midsummer, is celebrated on June 21st. It is the longest day, shortest night of the year. The Sun God is at his peak of power and preparing to give over his reign to the God of the Dark as winter approaches—but not first without a fight.

It's this time of year when the Oak King, representing the God of Summer, battles with the Holly King, representing the God of Winter. The Oak King is slain for the right of the Holly King to rule the upcoming dark half of the year. On the Winter

Solstice six months later, the two kings fight again, and the victorious Oak King rules the light once more. This ancient symbolic representation of the fight between the Solar Gods for power over the seasons of summer and winter is marked by the slow decline of light into darkness at the Summer Solstice after which the decline is more noticeable by the shortening of days and the lengthening of nights.

The full moon of the Summer Solstice is called "The Green Corn Moon" by the Cherokee Nation, "The Rose Moon" by the early American colonists, and "The Moon of Horses" by the Celtic people. By whichever name you call her, the full moon is eternally the moon of the Goddess; even if the Sun God holds power over the light of Midsummer, the Goddess still holds sway over the night.

The eve of the Summer Solstice was considered one of four special nights of the year when the veil between this world and the world of Faery was thin. The joy and revelry of the celebrations was enhanced by the moon, who lent her misty glowing light to those who were out and about, traveling back and forth within the two worlds.

This eve of Midsummer was the time when the Faery race collected certain kinds of fern seeds that helped render them invisible. Humans still go out on the eve of the Summer Solstice to collect these "spores" on the undersides of fern leaves, for ferns really have no seeds, per say, to collect. Supposedly, if you place one of these fern leaves inside your left shoe, it will help you attain the desired effect of invisibility. Of course, the Faeries really don't need to rely on fern seeds to render themselves invisible because their high energy vibration enables then to transcend time and space at will. You might want to give it a try yourself though, and see how it goes. You could find success in the form of disappearing hands or feet, and what an interesting experience that would be?!

Fire was an important custom honored on the eve of the Summer Solstice. Ritual bonfires were lit on hilltops. Torches were held aloft and whirled around in the air and carried in procession around the fields, and people drove their cattle between twin bonfires for protection—all to give honor to the dying sun god and render light into the approaching darkness.

The Salamanders were present for all the ancient fire festivals, as they are today. Whenever you light a match or use flint to start a fire, it's the Elemental Salamanders that animate the flame into being because this is their world: hot, mature, and passionate in nature, which is true power on the most primordial level.

Another way to call them forth is to first light a red candle that is facing south and then speak this invocation with reverence:

"Ancient Ones of the South, bringers of change and purification, illuminate the darkness with your sacred light and lend strength and passion to this rite. Help me find courage on my journey. You are honored at this circle. Welcome!"

When your rite is finished, remember to dismiss the Salamanders in a similar fashion with thanks of gratitude for adding their strength and protection to it, and then it is done.

An offering to the Salamanders on the day of the Summer Solstice or anytime you might want to contact them could be one of the fiery herbs previously discussed, like nettle or hawthorn. St. John's Wort is also said to cure melancholy moods if gathered on this day and can be dried and hung in a window to dispel negative forces entering your house, for it's also believed to keeps ghosts and other unsavory sorts away. To honor the Salamanders and draw them closer to you when you want to work with them, burn incense of frankincense, rosemary, or amber, for the slow burn of the pleasant-smelling incense will encourage them to pay attention to your summons by responding in a thoughtful compliant manner rather than a rash zealous one, which wouldn't be conducive to your magical undertakings.

Though stones are seen as belonging to the realm of the Gnomes rather than Salamanders, certain stones have a fire, air, and/or water element attached to them, too. Examples of this are chalcedony—the energy of water; malachite—the energy of Earth; and pumice—the energy of air. Asbestos, bloodstone, garnet, and diamond are a few of the stones associated with the fire element, so consider leaving one of these stones on your altar at Midsummer. Place it in a special area where the Salamanders will find it, like on the hearth of your fireplace or around the edge of a bonfire circle. Then the Elemental Salamanders will be prompted to work with you when these stones project their energy and attract their attention.

Dance is another medium that attracts Salamanders because a fast and frenzied dance builds up energy and will lure them to add their own strength and vitality to it. Traditionally, dancing was a magical act that sometimes revolved around a large bonfire in the center of the village and was accompanied by drumming. Some cultures used dance as a way to journey into altered states of consciousness to gain wisdom from their ancestors to help their people. For others, the object of dancing was to raise power for worship, to celebrate rites of passage, to honor the dead, or for prayer and magical workings. Dance is still utilized today to accomplish these same objectives.

Dancing in a circular formation, called the Round Dance by the pagan people, usually took place in a special area outdoors and was centered on a tree, stone, or a fire. This group dancing would raise energy and unite the group into a single focused purpose for accomplishing their goals.

The Maypole Dance is an old tradition that is still observed on May first. Its origins revolve around honoring the sacred marriage of the Sun God and the Earth Goddess, whose union ensures the continued growth and fertility of the land. The pole itself is a phallic symbol, representing the masculine aspect of the divine energies, while the earth is the feminine principle.

The Salamanders animate the spark of life-force in every living thing, so weaving together the streamers attached to the maypole was symbolic of weaving together the masculine and feminine sparks of life-force energy that controls the forces of life, death, and rebirth.

Fire is the eternal witness to sacred magical ceremonies and should always be left burning until it burns itself out, provided it can do so safely. Fire, also home to the Salamanders, symbolizes the very heart of a people and their connection to the higher powers, so dancing and fires form a physical expression of the spiritual element. Hand in hand, dancing and fires are part of the primal lifeforce within us that connects us to our past and who we are as incarnated beings.

Personal Sighting of an Elemental Salamander

When my father was eleven, he sighted an Elemental Salamander. This is his story, and I now respectfully pass it on to you.

I remember that I could hear the soft footsteps of my bare feet when they came in contact with the ground and compared them to my father's heavily booted ones as we walked alongside the cement irrigation ditch that skirted the road. His strides were longer; mine were more hurried, but he was a man, and I was yet a boy.

In the silent dark of evening with no moon to guide you, you know to *see* with your other senses:

How close are we to the creek? Smell.

Are we walking the upside of the levee yet? Touch.

"Hoo! Hoo!" from the owl perched in the gnarled oak tree that local legend said grew over the Faery's treasure of gold. Sound.

Tangy bitterness on our tongues from decaying willow leaves seeping into the mud and mingling with the air. Taste.

We're not alone in this darkness. The sixth sense—intuition.

We went slowly. In the dark you can do nothing else.

Our late start for home had been unavoidable, and now we were a mile into a very dark three-mile walk. In the dead of night, three miles is a long, long way. When you lived in the country in the 1930's, it meant that the chances of a car driving by and giving you a ride was slim to none. Not many people around there had cars or lived out that far.

So on we walked side by side, the sound of our breathing intensified by the quietness of the night. Off to my right, a misty orange glow like a pale defused ball of light caught my attention. It weaved and bobbed along like a stream of wind playing with an autumn leaf: forward, back, then around and around in a circle. Though it was a cool summer evening, beads of sweat were popping up on my forehead, and I felt slightly ill. I watched the orange light while it moved. As I did, my stomach felt strangely like a million butterflies had taken up residence, fluttering uncontrollably all the way up into my throat.

On we trudged in utter silence, focused on judging our steps in the dark though all the while I couldn't take my eyes from that mysterious light. I felt strangely possessed—like we were being led instead of followed—but follow us it did for another half-mile.

The path twisted to the right, and the big old oak tree appeared in front of us. I felt the urge to run but held myself in check instead. It seemed like my father hadn't spotted the light or was completely unconcerned, and I didn't want to appear timid.

Eventually, I couldn't hold back any longer, so I said in a whisper, "Dad, do you see it, the light?"

I touched him on the shoulder and saw his face, pale white against the night, turn towards me.

"There," I said. "Look. It's following us. What is it?"

He halted briefly, then grabbed hold of my shirt sleeve, pulling me forwards and said casually, "Oh, that's just a Jack O'Lantern," but I noticed we quickly picked up our pace and made a beeline for home.

As stated earlier in this chapter, some people call these mysterious lights St. Elmo's Fire, Jack O' Lanterns, or Will-O'-the-Wisps; however, by whatever name you choose to call them, it's well-advised not to tarry with them along your path at night because it's often debated as to whether they're friend or foe. Always proceed with caution and use a lot of common sense, for it is wise not to tempt anyone out on a moonless night, whoever (or whatever) it might be.

CHAPTER 4
West: The Realm of the Undines

L ast, but certainly not least, are the Undines, the Elementals that animate water. Their ruler is Necksa. Their alchemical symbol is an equilateral triangle pointed downward, which represents the water element with its cold and moist qualities that descend or condense. The colors associated with the Undines are all the varying shades of blue, from indigo to sky blue. West is their direction.

Down through time, west has been seen as the direction to the lands of the Ever-Young, what the Irish Celts called Tir na n'Og, a land beyond our own where life continues much the same only on a much more pristine level. This Blessed Realm was where everything eventually returned to, a bountiful land where the Gods, Faeries, and the Dead resided. This isle of peace and perfection was always reached by crossing a body of water, most specifically the sea, which was understood to be the gateway between our manifest world and the Otherworld, the land beyond time and space. It was the doorway through which one could access other levels of awareness and being, the portal from whence one could enter to visit the inhabitants of the Land of Faery.

The Undines are irresistible and seductive like the powerful primal sea herself, and they are the ones who fill it with life and action by helping keep our planet nourished and fertile. In the beginning, all life originated in this large body of water, which is considered to be the great womb of the Mother Goddess. It is also viewed as the ancient cauldron of creation, the waters of birth and transformation associated with the feminine principle and female energy, encompassing emotions like love, kindness, compassion, and empathy.

Many meanings and events are placed in the direction of west: autumn, Halloween, fertility, twilight, adulthood, creativity, and the moon. Healing, friendship, meditation, beauty, and love are goals associated with the direction of west. If you desire to have more loving relationships, become spiritually attuned, heal both physically and mentally, find or share love and beauty, then west would be the place used to accomplish these worthy goals. Working in the west helps us direct these towards fulfillment.

Since west is where autumn sits on the cyclical wheel of the seasons and the time of year we begin to slow down and prepare for the upcoming winter, it's a good time to start pulling back your energies and contemplating what you might need to accumulate to help you survive the coming onslaught of winter. What should you place in your larder, so to speak, to aid in your continued existence? Is it of a spiritual nature? Then the Undines can obviously help with the emotional aspects of that, for they rule emotions and the emotional plane and are connected energetically to that part of us as spirit in a human body. For some people, if it's of a physical nature like water, then the Undines can help there also, for water is the second most important element humans needed to survive. Since water is the greatest percentage of most living things, calling on the Undines would be the correct choice because they rule this fluid, changeable element and give the stimulation to quicken it for our consumption.

The three astrological signs of water are Cancer, Scorpio and Pisces. Their psychological mode is feeling, those ever elusive emotions that most of humanity tries to hide and ignore. It's hard to open ourselves up to truly feel and be vulnerable, but in the quest for balance, it's one requirement that cannot be overlooked. Being vulnerable doesn't mean being weak; it means being open and workable like clay and willing to allow life experiences to mold us into better more balanced versions of our human selves. It's through experiencing all aspects of the human emotions that we become who we innately are:

perfected beings that are centered, loving, and eternally part of the Higher Mind of the Creator.

The Cancer, Scorpio and Pisces personality is in tune with the waters of the great sea, ever linked to the ebbs and flows of the cycles of life. As such, they tend to be more consciously aware of the same ebbs and flows of emotions, adapting to what life brings their way. This doesn't mean that they can't dig in their heels and refuse to move, for stubbornness—aligned with temper—sometimes sneaks in, and their ability to be flexible flies out the window!

These three water signs, like the Elemental Undines, are deeply sensual and charming, able to move through life in a manner that seems Otherworldly to most. They are spiritually-minded and live harmoniously with the higher vibrational energies, bringing an awareness of these energies down to a more workable level for the rest of humanity. There are more spiritual leaders born under these three signs than any other, which attests to their innate ability to connect with the depths of spirit.

Their biggest challenges to overcome are moodiness and hypersensitivity. By establishing a relationship with the Undines, they can come to understand how to work with these two traits in a positive way and not become overwhelmed by them. They can call upon the energies of the Undines to wash away any negativity attached to them.

Cancer, Scorpio and Pisces people love deeply and tenderly and are dedicated when they find their life purpose. In addition, they are insightful, magnetic, and able to use their imagination to full advantage to connect them to the higher levels of consciousness to which they are so attuned. They explore levels of reality unseen or experienced by others because they are pathfinders through the tangled webs of life where eventually we all must follow, and we couldn't ask for better guides.

The Nature of Undines

There are many families of Undines inhabiting the ponds, waterfalls, rivers, fountains, and seas of earth, for all bodies of water are residences of the Elemental Undines who have been given names like Nymph, Naiad, Water Sprite, and Mermaid. They generally appear in human form, usually female—though there are plenty of male Undines—and are extremely beautiful and seductive. Their movements are fluid and graceful and are said to evoke strong emotions in those they encounter. Their skin has a pale bluish tint, their hair is long, their eyes are dark, and their touch is cool and moist.

Undines can be hard to control because of their fluid nature, which is always moving, changing, and difficult to pin down, but they are usually friendly towards humans. They are passionate, loving, and not afraid of playing on these emotions in others to get their way. People tend to shy away from their emotions, but emotions are one of the tools that we're given to learn what it is to be an incarnated human, so the Undines can help us learn more about emotions and the emotional states of the conscious and unconscious mind by showing us that it's all right to love deeply, be sad, mourn, rejoice, act silly, cry, and be vulnerable. Also, they can assist us in recognizing our shadow side—the side of us that is not always pleasant and balanced—and work with it to better understand those prickly bits and not let them rule us.

If not addressed, our shadow side is like a dark pool that draws us in with promises of refreshment but overwhelms us with the heaviness of the sludge called denial if we don't recognized that side of us first and do something to heal it. The Undines can dredge out those shadowy sediments; tapping into our unconscious minds and helping us map the path to emotional holism while bringing balance to our lives. In turn, this will eventually bring the whole world back into balance—one person at a time.

Undines like anything associated with water: shells, lily pads, icebergs, coral and pearls, willow trees, tide pools, rain, geysers, fog and most especially those deep dark unexplored depths of seas and lakes—those mysterious places where the Undines hide. They enjoy playing in the colorful rainbows of tiny water droplets, riding on top of giant waves out at sea, flying through the air on an ice crystal, and banging on metal rooftops in a storm. They like the smell of a fresh spring rain, the sound of a waterfall as it cascades over the edge of a cliff, and the sight of happy tears on a loved one's face. Wherever you'll find water is where you'll find the Elemental Undines in their many phases and moods, just waiting for humans to contact them.

If you want to get the attention of an Undine, place a water fountain or pond in your yard, mist your houseplants well, and/or chase your children through a sprinkler in summer just for fun. If you place your hand over a puddle of water, you'll feel the Undines as they send their vibrational energy to you, for they are resonating with the fluids in your body, and it's these fluids that the Undines control to a certain degree.

The Elemental Undines live on the invisible side of nature and govern the emotional body of humanity/our emotional state. They'll help us tune into our psychic mind and emotional spirituality, for our psychic mind is the place we receive information other than the usual, information through precognition, telepathy, clairvoyance, dreams, etc., which can assist us in forming new positive thought patterns and connections with the natural world—thus moving us up in evolution. The psychic mind is a direct channel to the One, the Higher Mind of the Creator. We are all capable of tapping into this channel; it's just a matter of training and practicing. By connecting and working with the Undines and allowing them to assist us, we can nurture this link with the One and let the knowledge from the collective unconscious flow into our psychic center, opening it up for attaining a stronger positive emotional outlook on life and the future of the planet, which rests in our hands as stewards of the earth.

Gifts and offerings that the Elemental Undines enjoy are herbs like Irish Moss, Violet, Rose, Lilac, Grape, or Aster sprinkled into a creek or spring. Collect a leaf on the riverbank, place some ground rose petals or violet flowers in the middle of it, and carefully send it floating downstream with your prayers of thanks for your newly acquired understanding of the Undines. As a votive offering, you could also take a silver coin or small silver object to a well or natural spring and toss it into the water in gratitude.

Silver is a metal of the emotions, the Goddess, and the Moon that rules the waters of earth. It's well remembered that if you throw a coin into a well or fountain while making a wish, your wish will be granted in no time at all. Not only will you get the attention of the Undines, but wells are access points down into the earth, so the Elemental Gnomes can be included in your offering.

Calling on the Elemental Undines is helpful when you want to work on the emotional aspects of your psyche, so if emotions are something you keep locked up out of fear of being unable to handle them, draw the alchemical symbol of water over a bowl of water and place it in the west of your altar. You can also draw it on a piece of paper with a blue felt pen and place it underneath the water bowl. Then ask for their assistance in coming to terms with these emotions and leave it there from the new moon to the new moon. Remember to replenish the water as needed. You can also invoke them during ritual work and ask for their help by using this prayer or one of your own:

Elementals of water, sacred ones of the West where the ancient priestesses of Avalon dwell, bring to me the deep psychic energies I need to heal my emotions. Lend me the power of the Priestess of Healing to heal my own emotional state. Bring me wisdom and insight in my endeavors to clarify what is useful in my quest for balance and what is unhealthy for me. Join me, Friends from the West. Welcome.

Lift up your arms to the west and thank the powers that reside there.

Water scrying is another way in which the Undines can assist us, for they are of this fluid, ubiquitous element and can give us the power to achieve vision through this means. Scrying is the practice of gazing into something reflective like a bowl of water, a crystal sphere, or a mirror to obtain clairvoyant sight.

When scrying with water, a black bowl filled with natural spring or rainwater will benefit the person doing the scrying better than tap water because when you work in any magical venue, it is always by using the purest natural elements that our goals are achieved.

Once the bowl is filled, set it in a dimly lit room with a soft light behind you but reflected slightly in the water. Now gaze into the water keeping your eyes relaxed, for there's no need to strain and make them sore or burn; just look intently but comfortably. Your scrying bowl should eventually mist over, and you'll begin to see dim shadowy figures, objects, or symbols. After a certain amount of practice, the images will become clearer, brighter, and more natural. Sometimes you will see images in the bowl, sometimes you will see them in your mind's eye, and sometimes both; however they come, remember to trust what your intuition tells you about them. By working with the Elemental Undines in this fashion, you will be able to chart your lifecourse in a direction that is more conducive to your own balanced objectives.

Water is reflective like a looking glass, and the Elemental Undines can reflect back to us our own true image and destiny. They will strive to stimulate our emotional plane, help us absorb positive life experiences, and link us to our dream state where we, as humans, can work out our deepest longings and fears. Undines are versatile, just like water, so open up and let them flow into your life with all the unique assistance they're so willingly to give us.

The Autumn Equinox

O God of the Sea, put weed in drawing wave to enrich the ground, to shower on us food!

On September 21st, day and night are of equal lengths. We prepare for a stronger push towards winter as the sun appears to grow even weaker by the passing of days. Nature slowly recedes into the earth while the nights grow colder, and all of life gradually looks towards the time for bundling up and resting in the arms of our Mother Earth. September days are still warm, the harvest is being savored, and the autumn leaves fall lazily to the earth in fluttering waves of red and gold. Bright orange pumpkins smile up at us from their resting-place on the ground, and lizards lie drowsing on nearby rocks enjoying the warmth of the sun.

On this date of the autumn equinox, the Celtic god Mabon, the son of Modron can be remembered. Mabon was a sun god among the tribes of Britain and called the Divine Youth, the Son of Light. He was the mysterious lost god of many names who vanished at his birth but was eventually found in an Underworld castle where he had been imprisoned. When he was finally released, he emerged as a young hero and champion who brought vigor and eternal life to humanity.

The full moon of September is called "The Harvest Moon" or "The Barley Moon" and is celebrated by the harvesting of grain that the earth provides. The Celts call it "The Singing Moon," which in one aspect relates to the melodious songs of the Undines, who are known to possess voices so beautiful and enchanting that they can even put the angel's singing to shame. If you listen to the echoes of the sea, you'll understand the irresistible pull that draws people to the great open waters of the oceans of the world. The perpetual swish-boom of breakers hitting the rocks, the reverberation of sound drifting inwards as you stand on shore watching the horizon, and the din of sea spray rising into the air are the hypnotic voices of the Undines resonating inside your body and leading you back to your primordial blood, back home. They wait for you there in the salty waves and misty fog that hovers over the landscape, in the silvery haze of the moon in the distant night sky, and in the gentle rhythms of the tides as they move back and forth with the turnings of this moon, for they are waiting for you to respond to the call of the ancient boundless sea, so listen. Listen, for they're ever near, calling.

Other offerings you can give the Undines might be small pieces of apple, melon, or cherry left beside a river or the shores of the sea. You can cast a water element stone of Aquamarine or Moonstone into a stream or lake to honor the energy of the Undines, saying prayers to the Water Goddesses Venus, Isis, Sequana, Yemanya, or Sedna while doing so.

To attract the attention of the Elemental Undines by showing reverence to one of the Water Goddesses whose protection they are under, place a bowl of water on your altar with periwinkle or narcissus flowers floating in it, extend your projective hand (whichever hand is your dominate one) over the bowl and say:

Great Goddess of the Primal Waters, Mistress of the Moon, protector of the Elemental water spirits, help me to cut the dimness between the worlds and open love and knowledge to all your children on earth so that we may reconnect with your power and see with true eyes what others choose not to see.

Then dip the index and middle finger on your receptive hand into the water (the hand which is opposite your projective hand) and bring them first to your forehead between your eyebrows—the third eye—and say, "I anoint my eyes to see her."

Next bring these two fingers to your lips and say, "My lips to speak her name," then to your heart and say, "And my heart to hold her in my love."

Afterward, leave the bowl of water there on your altar for three days. When the days are past, take the water outside, and with words of thanks, pour it onto the earth while facing west, and know your prayer has been heard.

Music and singing are equally important to the Undines. Starting a personal relationship with them could include playing music with a water theme, like George Handel's *Water Music*, or Franz Schubert's *Songs on the Theme of Water*. Other good sounds combining nature with music are brought together by NorthSound and include composers like Mozart, Gershwin, Pachelbel, and Nature's Drums. Try learning to play the Glass Harmonica, a favorite of Renaissance Fairs, by using glass bowls or goblets filled with water and rubbing your wet finger along the rim, which will produce a one-tone musical note. By using several bowls or goblets you can create music that some have called "The Voices of Angels."

By learning and understanding how to connect with the Elemental Undines and honoring the direction and season with which they are associated, you can begin your path towards working with these last Elementals who are one on the wheel of four: Earth, Air, Fire, and Water consecutively. So congratulations and may all your magical pursuits be successful!

Lakes and ponds are entryways into the Otherworld, as well as dreams, for dreams connect us with the realm of the Undines and the road to the collective unconscious, a source of knowledge which is shared within all of us and links our unconscious mind, our intuition, with our conscious mind, our waking mind. We can balance the conscious with the unconscious by blending our intuition with our emotional state, providing us with a rich inner resource from which to dip. Undines will often manifest through our dream state in order to get our attention and to help us further our work here. This story is an encounter with an Elemental Undine that I experienced through the Dreamtime.

A Dreamtime Encounter with an Undine

Skimming over the smooth glassy surface of a large lake I flew, cradling my loved one in my arms. A green mountainous countryside surrounded the sun-kissed lake and sent tiny blue-green lights shimmering across the water. Pure fresh air swept by, carried on the warm summer current of a breeze, and I breathed deeply the intoxicating aroma.

Happiness and contentment bubbled inside of me as I enjoyed the wind on my face, the freedom of flight, and my love for the one I held in my arms, for at that moment I had no cares in the world.

Well, out over the middle of the lake, I glanced downward and saw to my surprise and apprehension a man's face, beautiful in appearance but strange to see as he swam looking up, watching us while I flew above in the air, only four fingers' breadth away. The water was as clear as crystal, and I could see every detail below, every rock and grain of sand, the scales on the fish swimming by, the algae green bottom of the lakebed, and his smooth white flesh and long black hair drifting at his feet that partially covered his naked body. I strained my eyes towards the horizon and flew faster, but the faster I flew, the more he kept up. A surge of fear shot through me. I was unsure what to expect, but suddenly I stopped short because he rose up out of the water in front of me while my stomach took a couple of turns, and I held my breath.

There were no sounds now—only the three of us face to face. A smile parted his lips as he raised his hands to produce a protective bubble around our bodies. It flashed in pale colors of white, gold, and blue, and I calmed instantly. Then he moved away, sliding back down into the lake, shrinking below and disappearing into nothingness as my soul found perfect peace once again.

With knowledge certain, as if a door to the sun had suddenly cracked open, I knew that he was a water Elemental come to show me the strengths and powers of his kind's manifestations within water, for he was a ruler over the deep lakes and ancient waters of the peaceful watery realms to the Otherworld—the land of Tir na n'Og where all the Elemental spirits reside.

CHAPTER 5
Ritual and Magic

Ritual has been described as a sequence of actions we use to attach ourselves more deeply to the sacred and the divine. Ritual helps us journey towards a spiritual awakening and connects us to the realms of the Otherworld. It is through ritual that we tap into the powers that assist us in accomplishing our magical goals.

The forces of the Otherworld are much more dominate in those whose spiritual heritage comes from that oft unseen dimension, but anyone can learn to work with this energy by means of the ritual process. These Otherworld forces are seen not through a narrow vision of the human experience. Instead, they are seen through a wider consciousness dedicated to the evolution of humanity by bringing knowledge back from this other dimension in order to make changes in our reality.

Different religions or traditions use various tools in performing rituals to achieve altered states of consciousness, which directly connects them to the Higher Powers of their tradition. Sweet grass, candles, crosses, incense, tobacco, robes, and water are just some of the items that help us focus our energies and intentions to bring about a desired outcome, for these things help us to separate the base or ordinary from the sacred or divine.

Ritual can be used to celebrate the great cycles of the sun and moon, the passing of the seasons, the passing of the phases of human life and/or to gain assistance for maintaining the balance and health of the planet, for magical goals, and as a show of appreciation for life itself. Whatever our reason for doing ritual, it needs to be an attitude that we carry with us from day to day, an attitude to recognize the sacred in everything and be grateful for it. Not only do we receive, but we should also remember to give back in gratitude.

From the very beginning of thinking what you wish to celebrate or accomplish in regards to holding a specific ritual—your purpose and intent—you've already begun the process. Holding the thought first in your mind energizes the power to accomplish your goals and sends out your intent to those you wish assistance from. From that moment forward, all the rest is basic. You just need to put your own personal spin to it.

All people have their own form and approach to ritual. Bathing as an act of purification and preparation can begin the focus, for it is always better to begin a ritual cleansed, which also includes having a clear mind and clear idea of your intention. A bath in the privacy of your own home (or if you're lucky enough to have the opportunity to do this outdoors) will cleanse anything you don't want to carry into your ritual working space. Don't forget to say prayers to the spirits of the water element in gratitude for their cleansing and healing energies. Water is the blood of the Earth Goddess who takes the negative and base energy from our experiences in life and washes them away through the bathing process to return that cleansed negative energy back to the planet as positive energy for the benefit of all.

Next is creating a sacred space in which to work your ritual. First, establish a center where you can focus your intent. Start from a place of stillness within your body and then move outward into your material mundane space. By first holding that stillpoint within, you will have free reign to draw those energies to you because it creates balance, both inside and out. Magic and ritual is much more effective when everything is balanced, including the elements of Earth, Air, Fire, and Water.

Here is an exercise that can be used to balance those energies:

1)   Draw a circle on the ground that extends to the length of your outstretched arm, about 30". If you're outdoors, you can draw this circle with a stick or staff. Indoors, you can use the same staff and visualize the circle being drawn in blue

light, or you can use a charcoal stick on the floor where it's safe to do so. (Test the area first to make sure you can remove it easily.)

2)	In the center of the circle, draw a pentagram—a five-pointed star inside a circle. The star's five points represent the four elements of life, plus spirit (quintessense) or the Fifth Element, which is the lifeforce element itself. The circle represents the body of humankind. The pentagram should be drawn with one point upwards—in this instance, east—where the point of the quintessense rules over the other four elements. It represents the Higher Mind ruling over the world of matter. This is where you will sit when balancing the four Elemental energies.

3)	In the north of your circle, place a small bowl of earth. In the east, place an air-filled jar that has set outside on a windy day. (This jar should be capped after being outside.) In the south, place a lit red candle, and in the west, place a bowl of water.

4)	Sit in the center of your circle on the pentagram facing east. Extend your dominant hand over the air jar. Visualize spiritual energy coming down through your crown chakra into your extended arm and hand and then down into the jar of air. When you feel the palm of your hand getting heavier, close off this energy by thinking it closed and then turn to the south. Do the same exercise for each of the other three elements, turning in a sunrise direction. (Be careful not to get too close to the flame of the candle and burn the palm of your hand.)

5)	Once you're back facing east, sit quietly with eyes closed and see in your mind's eye the four Elemental energies drifting near you. Is one heavier than the others? Are any on the verge of disappearing all together? Match the texture, density, and taste of each element with your own four bodily elements and "see" by visualizing which needs attending to. Take any energies that are lacking and visually fill them up from the four elemental tools that you just charged: bowl of earth, candle flame, etc., and then take any that are too dense and siphon them off, sending the extra energy out into your charged tools.

6)   Check again through your visualization and feel the Elemental energies around you. Trust what you see and feel. Are they radiating in tune with each other? Good.

7)   Through your mind's eye again—your visualization— weave these four Elemental energies together into a balanced tapestry of light and love. Call upon the magic inside you, your own four Elemental energies, and pull the amount needed to balance the area where you will do your ritual. Once you feel the area around you balanced, open your eyes and know that it is done.

When you're practiced enough, you won't need to use the physical representations of each element (i.e., candle flame, water, earth, air jar) unless you desire, for you can visualize and use your own energies to pull from. The physical tools used in any ritual just help in focusing will and intent, for humans are visual creatures by nature and seem to need these props to keep the mind from wandering, which works quite well. You can also use this exercise to balance any area you wish: home, yard, picnic area, work space, campground, etc.

Think of your sacred space as the ever protective and nourishing womb of the Goddess where you're held and given a place to grow, evolve, and then birth your desires. It's where the regenerative powers of the Divine burn within each one of us, and when birthed through visualization, they resemble the aurora borealis in its entire brilliant splendor, energetically brought into the realm of the ritual working space.

Assuming you have already chosen a place in which to hold your rite—maybe outdoors in a forest, in your own back yard, or indoors somewhere—make sure it is a place you feel perfectly safe. It doesn't do to feel uncomfortable or anticipate being interrupted because that will take away from your focused goal. If you do feel more comfortable inside, make sure ringing telephones or unsuspecting family members walking in at inopportune moments won't disturb you. It's moments like those that can squelch a ritual pretty darn fast, so let everyone know beforehand that you need quiet and solitude unless they plan on joining you.

Creating a physical sacred space involves channeling energy from the Divine-Source down through your crown chakra and up from below through the energy center openings of your feet. Use your solar plexus energy as well by matching and mingling it with the vibrations coming through your crown and feet chakras, thus creating a cohesive energy current with which to work.

Working with energy is a matter of knowledge and usage when looking to achieve your magical goals. Constituent substance/matter is nothing more than energy vibrating at different levels or speeds. The higher this matter vibrates, the more ethereal it appears—like spirit; the lower it vibrates, the denser it appears—like rocks. Once the vibration is high enough, it will vibrate right out of our own density range until we can no longer see it. Humans are attuned to a third-dimensional vibration, so that is the level we generally operate from even though everything in creation shares the same space.

In the end we come to understand that everything that ever was, is, or will be is ultimately of the same energy and connected on a deeper vibrational level than we can visually see. Even though you can't see energy or vibration with your physical eyes doesn't mean it doesn't exist. You can't see radio waves, right? But push the button on your radio, and voilà, you've got juice. It's the same with magical energy workings.

It's humans that take the currents or energy from the earth and run it through the chakras of the body to send out to a given purpose, for we are the conduits of that electrical power, and ritual is the connection with that part of the energy of Divine creation. Working with energy is about visualization and placing your intent, your focus, so finding an experienced and knowledgeable teacher who can guide you into the realms of magic and ritual with confidence and perspective is a must. Magic can be slippery if you're unprepared. The power that's required in working with magic and energy manipulation isn't something to blindly jump into, for the true study and practice of magic is ultimately about developing the power to aid in your own evolution and growth, which in the end aids in the evolution of humanity.

Next comes an invocation to welcome the Deities, and then you work the ritual. This is always followed by releasing the energy you've raised from the rite. All that's left is the offerings of thanks and the closing of the sacred circle, which is usually followed by eating and drinking something to ground yourself back to earth.

As stated before, this book is about understanding the Elemental and Nature Spirits, not specifically how to work a magical ritual, so again, a good teacher is essential if it's more magical aspects you desire to learn.

The Elements and their counterparts are essential on any spiritual path and are necessary for the successful practice of magic, for they can provide new understandings and give us the power to accomplish. They'll show us the mystery and sacredness of the world and the hidden forces of nature in which magicians work. Each element corresponds to what is called the Four Powers of the Magus, which are to know, to dare, to will, and to be silent. To know corresponds to the air element. To dare corresponds to the water element. To will corresponds to the fire element, and to be silent corresponds to the earth element. By getting to know and working with the Gnomes of earth, Sylphs of air, Salamanders of fire, and Undines of water, you'll learn how important they truly are for the continuation and regeneration of creation. We need to be fully committed to doing our part to help maintain the health of the planet, for we are all stewards of this earthly garden of divinity, and it is our sacred duty to them, the earth, and to each other to do so.

Kiss The Wind

INTRODUCTION
The Faery Folk

If you asked ten people whether there's a difference between Elementals and Faeries, you'd get ten different answers, for everyone has an opinion about such matters. But if you asked a magician or alchemist, they'd most likely tell you it's the Elementals that are employed in magical operation, not the Faeries. The Elementals were involved in the first acts of creation, for they were the ones who stimulated this creative effort into action. Magicians and alchemists still relate to them through their power to animate. Most people classify both groups as being of the same caste though, so for easier reference in this section, we'll group them together as such, remembering that the Elementals create and the Faery beings sustain.

The Faeries, as a whole, are intelligent beings that are close to humans in evolution but more ethereal and refined than us, for they have bodies that are light, pliable, and subtle, unlike our more dense human bodies that vibrate at a slower rate. The Faeries were created just after the earth and are the caretakers of the natural world. They are magical beings who reside in a different dimension than ours, one the Celtic tradition called the "Otherworld." This Otherworld is a place neither here nor there but a betwixt and between realm where beats the pulse of the creative force.

In the Celtic countries of Ireland, Scotland and Wales, the Faery beings are an integral part of the mythology of the land. The doorway to the Otherworld was sometimes referred to as the Door with No Key, or the Oaken Door because it was a strong and powerful portal into the dwelling places of the gods, ancestors, and the dead—those illustrious beings that live by their own free will beyond this spiritual portal. These ancient gods were called the Sidhe/Sith, or People of the Mounds in Ireland and Scotland, and Tylwyth Teg or the Fair Family in

Wales. The name, Sidhe, is now synonymous with the hills, mounds, and cairns where these beings dwell across much of Western Europe. Some say that over time the Christian Church downgraded the gods from god status to Faery status and branded them as fallen angels, not worthy enough to enter heaven but not wicked enough to enter hell. Still others feel that because of the ongoing disbelief in them, the ancient gods turned Faery and have continued to lessen in the minds and hearts of the people, so they feel they are no longer relevant and have vanished because of this. In reality, the old gods are just as powerful and present now as they ever were, but they remain hidden from mortal sight for reasons of their own choosing. This revolves, in part, around the fact that humanity has detached themselves from the natural world and the knowledge that life on this planet works together as a whole cohesive unit with no one thing or any another being better or more evolved.

The doorway into the Otherworld where the gods/Faeries live is a portal that leads symbolically to the spiritual realm inside each and every one of us and is accessed normally when communing with Source or Creator. Entry to the Otherworld is available through various means: a) the dreamtime or other altered states of consciousness, such as meditation or journeying; b) at in-between places, like a fork in the road or the edge of a sea; c) seasonal cross-quarter times, like Samhain and Beltaine when the veil between the worlds of humans and Otherworld residents is thin; d) at natural places in nature like springs, caves, and deep in the forests; e) and during rituals when these entryways are closer due to the sensitive nature of ritual work. We can travel back and forth into Faery, as it's sometimes called, by using our imagination and ability to dream and visualize. It's these abilities that open the door, enabling us to converse with Otherworld beings and bring wisdom from that consciousness into our own to help make things better for everyone residing on this planet.

Some people can see the Faeries directly with what's called the Second Sight, which is a term used to describe the psychic ability to look beyond the surface world into the spiritual world of the Faeries beings or the Otherworld. Those with the Second Sight often have other gifts as well, such as the gift of vision (seeing past, present or future events), clairaudience (being able to receive impressions of sound, music and voices), or the gift of healing by touch. These psychic abilities generally run in families, but everyone possesses these abilities and has an inherent knowledge on how to develop them if taught the correct procedures for doing so.

The existence of the Otherworld is not a modern concept; instead, it is an ancient time-spanning tradition to which folklore, hereditary spiritual practices, and long standing cultural beliefs attest. We can again become conscious co-creators with the denizens of Faery by journeying there if we desire and understand how to do so. It can be a tricky path though because the Fae are not too pleased with us, for we've been steadily destroying their world—the world of nature— and because of our disregard for its sacred and divine aspects and the fact that we've separated ourselves from it, they've come to consider us selfish, arrogant, disrespectful, and untrustworthy. Who can blame them, for have we not proven this to be so?

For far too long, humanity has either ignored or mistreated the natural world, so we're now being compelled to learn to nurture and heal what we've wounded and bring balance back to our earth and its slowly diminishing resources; however, first we need to awaken from our self-imposed slumber and see the world as it's become—one that's drowning in the destructive search for power and control at all costs, which is reflected in our abuse of the planet. It's among these issues where we'll find what is eating away at our very core and destroying us from within.

Humans have watched the blatant slaughter of nature with only a passing wince of the eye, not willing to accept responsibility for what they've done. This has gone on so long that the Faery beings have almost given up hope on us ever realizing there's a major problem and finding the ways and means to fix it.

All is not lost though, for in learning to access the land of Faery and helping bring balance back into the world by working with the Faery beings, we'll also learn how to heal our own personal wounds. This is a big step towards holism and a bigger step towards balancing our feelings of separation from the earth with our misplaced desire to dominate it. To help us understand what this entails, we first need to clarify what is and is not *Faery*.

Faery can be a place, as well as a being. The word *Faery* comes to us by way of the French word *fée* (pronounced fay) and is derived from the Latin word *fatare*, meaning "to enchant" and Fates, the goddesses who rule the destinies of humankind. The world of Faery exists right here beside us in a dimension beyond our own, not in some far-off place of fantasy and make-believe.

The Faeries you'll encounter on your path through the Otherworld are just as diversified in looks and temperaments as humans are in this world. Some are friendly and some can be hostile. Some are short and stout and some are tall or even taller than humans and of a willowy stature, but that in itself also depends on how you expect to see them because they're highly inclined to pick an image out of your imagination and run with it, for they don't have the same sense of feelings humans do and find this game an amusing pastime.

Some are happy and some you'll find are just as well left alone, but of all they are or are not, one thing's sure: you'll never run across a real Faery with butterfly wings sprinkling pixie dust around. The idea of winged Faeries started with the Victorian Era and its insatiable taste for embellishment. The Victorians felt if something was good, like Faeries, then adding something more, like gossamer butterfly wings seemed better all around. In reality, the Faeries of our ancestors never had nor needed wings because their energy was of a higher vibration than most everything else and enabled them to move through the dimensions of time and space at will, so why would they need wings to travel? But again, if that's the way you expect to see them, chances are you will.

The old original word *Faery* was used to describe powerful nature and fertility spirits of great wisdom and age, but over time the word was misapplied until it seemed to diminish these powerful beings in stature and importance by the very word itself. Today the Faeries of our world are considered to be nothing more than children's tales of cute little winged cherubs whose only goal is to play in gardens and make humans happy.

The Elven Folk

Beliefs about the Elven Folk have also changed throughout history. Early Norse mythology tells us that after their death in battle, men could rise to the high rank of Elves, which was a great honor in light of the elevated status they held among the general population. Elves were considered the oldest created beings on this planet and were here long before time began. They have had common children with humans, and the children of these unions were said to be more beautiful than others because of their Elven blood. Many of the nobility in the German and Scandinavian countries claimed Elf ancestry so were not bound to normal human laws, being autonomous instead, and not given to obeying the common law of the land. The Elves were a caste all their own, having great strength, size, beauty, wisdom and never consider Faeries in the modern sense of the word, but here we'll place them within that context as well.

Faeries are of the earth and the wild natural places. They don't stand apart from the world of nature because they are the world of nature, dwelling mostly invisible to humans who readily refuse to see them. In spite of our blindness, they are ever present among us, for they can come and go at will and are never confined to one place, being able to travel wherever they chose in the blink of an eye. If they do decide to befriend you, which a lot of the time they won't, you'll have a special ally to assist you throughout your life—or until they decide to turn you loose, for Faery beings can be very temperamental and difficult to understand because their lives are governed by an entirely different set of rules.

The Fae are drawn to people who are artistic and imaginative like they are. They can reward a favored human with creative gifts, such as music, painting, poetry, writing, and storytelling if they've grown to trust that human and found that person worthy of such gifts. Do take care to not cross the Faeries though, or you may find yourself waking up in an empty cornfield with all your worldly possessions vanished into the mists, for the Faery folk live in a world of enchantment where nothing's as it seems, the unusual is commonplace, and Faery magic continues to hold power.

Whatever the nature and temperament of the Faery beings, their world mirrors ours and reflects an image of what our world can be again with their cooperation. Because of humanity's increasing disconnection from and abuse of the natural world, our worlds slowly drifted apart. At the beginning they were both in alignment with each other, but it wasn't the Faeries that moved away. It was we who steadily shifted our focus from them, and the separation occurred— much to the detriment of all.

If you do decide to take up the mantel in defense of nature and the earth and go with an open heart and a desire to right the wrongs that have been inflicted upon it, you've taken the first step towards being accepted by the Faeries and maybe convincing them to work with us again as they once did. Though the passage of time has been extensive since we were all in cooperation, they are still a strong and proud race who is close to the earth and ever hopeful that humanity can change in spite of what we've done.

Humans' Experiences with Faeries

Five of the stories in this section are from my own experiences. One is a tale I heard as a child, and the other is my father's encounter with the Faery beings. The symbolism and meanings of the situations in which they manifested is at the beginning of each story. All are written with permission from my Faery allies and the participants who are still incarnate.

My hope in sharing these experiences is that the readers will come to an understanding that there are innumerable seen and unseen beings that rely on the green and growing things of nature. They're concerned about what happens here, and so should we be. Humans must take better care of what sustains us all, which is this big round ball in space, our Mother Earth.

Let's honor the earth and remember that though we may not always see them, the Faeries are everywhere—waiting among the open fields and deep in the forests, hiding in the windswept seas or behind a cover of clouds, resting upon the brightness of a sunbeam or in the hollow hills. Wherever you may encounter them, always be courteous and remember to take the time to listen, for wisely they speak in soft voices . . . and you wouldn't want to miss the extraordinary experience of being able to live the legends, would you?

The Bid of the Crone

As I sat in my kitchen looking out the window and sipping a cup of hot chocolate, I watched the crows flying along with the current of winter air. I could hear their cries as they flung themselves across the sky, dipping below the gray clouds in chase of each other. They seemed to tag and fly in the opposite direction just for fun, and I was enjoying watching their play.

The evergreens that edged my yard were making a barrier against the coming storm though occasionally they'd bend and sway as if stretching to hear their names whispered along the edge of the wind.

While I watched, nature showed herself in the guise of Crone, the Wise Dark One, the Lady of Winter who slowly goes dormant this time of year to patiently await rebirth in spring. She appeared more baffling and unpredictable than usual though, which sent me into the quiet of my own inner space for cover and to seek comfort among the Faery beliefs of my ancestors.

Even if we've closed our eyes to the gods and Faeries and no longer believe in them, they continue to make music here and tend to the needs of the earth like they did so long ago. Once they lived here on our surface world working to sustain it, and they still do, but now they're quiet and invisible, weaved like air into the landscape as they wait for us to remember them again. Their intention is the same as always: to animate the planet with the energy and substance needed for keeping it healthy and in balance for future generations.

The Faery folk live, laugh, and love much the same as we do, but now they're only distant fading memories relegated to myth and legend as our inner vision faded and our worlds slowly drifted apart. And so this question remains: "Is anyone left who wants to listen to the tales of the Old Ones any longer, those magical beings who dwell hidden among the lands where we reside?" It seems that for us the pursuits of the manifest world have overshadowed what can and should be learned from the lands where the ancient ones dwell because we seem to have closed our eyes to the secrets of nature and became "civilized"—no longer trusting what our ancestors innately knew through living close to the land.

The Faeries are present in the cold, frozen times of winter, as well as the warm brightness of spring, and on and out into every minute of every month of the year if we'll just pause long enough to take the time to look. But just now, while we're all tucked up in our warm beds with the covers thrown over our heads trying to hide from winter, we can learn to expand our awareness by getting up and stealing out into the forests in search of those who dwell there, for certainly they do because I know them, and the chapters that follow share a few of their stories.

CHAPTER 6
The Story of the Trooping Faeries

Beltaine and Favored Faery Trees

May first is Beltaine, one of four Celtic holy days that was considered *a time of no time* when the door between the worlds was thrust open and the inhabitants freely ventured forth, for it was then that the Faeries took their leave of Faeland and roamed the countryside wearing hawthorn flowers in their hair. The hawthorn, oak, and ash trees were sacred to the Faeries. It was said that if these were growing together, the Faeries could be sighted there. The white flowers and red berries of the hawthorn were two primary colors of the Otherworld and the Sidhe, the old Irish gods turned Faery.

As observed in the Old and New World Faery tradition, thorn trees, or hawthorns, were used in bringing visions, respectfully calling forth the Faery beings and working magically with Otherworld forces. A lone hawthorn on a hilltop or at a crossroad was said to be a doorway leading into the Faery realm and called the Faery's Trysting Tree, which was never tampered with for fear of retaliation in offending the Faeries. The hawthorn was also honored as a tree of the Earth Goddess in her state as maiden, for in winter her berries came full and red—the bleeding time—as she waited to mate with the God in spring, bringing forth new life on earth, which the Faeries have a hand in growing and nurturing.

The redbud is America's own indigenous Faery tree. This North American native flowers at the end of winter and cheerfully heralds the coming of warmer weather with its edible pink flowers and heart shaped leaves. It's no wonder the Faeries have chosen it as one of their own, for it always brings a smile to all that encounter it.

Seers say that the Faeries love to dance around the redbud at twilight and make special appearances on the eve of Beltaine in celebration of spring. If you want to make a good impression, hang wind chimes in the branches and wait for the soft music to whisper through like the sound of the sweet voiced Faeries themselves.

Faeries also love the world's tallest trees, redwoods, which are guardians and overseers of the forest and sacred to those who practice tree magic. In a redwood grove, there is always one tree that stands as a sentinel for the whole. This is usually the largest and oldest tree in the group, but not always. Get to know the redwoods and form a relationship with them, and you'll become aware which tree this is. Treefolk energy is gentler and easier to work with than the other vibrational energies of nature because trees truly desire to get to know humans and teach them how nature functions.

Redwoods are also the oldest growing trees in the world outside of the European Yew, which are said to live 4,000 years, but that number is difficult to prove because they regenerate themselves from their decaying centers. Some California redwoods were known to be 2,200 years old, and some Sequoias 3,200 years, but most redwoods live an average of 500-700 years.

A redwood grove can serve as a portal into another time and place by energetically opening up a doorway and providing the inhabitants of either place direct access for moving back and forth between the inner dimensions of these two realities. They are choice trees for working with the higher powers and drawing those powers down to earth. Merging with nature and animals are also powers the redwood trees can offer us because they are associated with the Elemental earth Gnomes who are their guardians. Our earthly realm is one way you can travel to connect with the dwelling places of the Faeries, and redwoods can help blend our energy with this most solid and balanced element.

The Norse god of thunder, lightning, and storms, Thor, is also connected with the redwood, for the redwood reaches upward, ever striving towards the heavenly realms where this power is manifested. It's the redwood tree that can give us protection and insight for moving forward in our lives, for they are so tall they can see from a higher perspective which direction is best for us to go and provide us clear unrestrained vision.

Beltaine is a time to celebrate spring and rebirth. It's a sacred day set apart to honor fertility, sexuality, action, and the rising heat beginning at the start of the summer season. This is the time the earth is giving new life to her nature children, so parties, feasting, and love among the haystacks under a crisp May moon are just the things to celebrate this special time.

The Faeries are conscious of the festival of Beltaine, which is why they choose to come forth from their Otherworld home into ours. It is a symbolic rebirth of spring because they are, in fact, nature spirits who help the plant life grow and thrive.

It is said that on those nights when the veil between the worlds is thin, the Trooping Faeries ride out into our surface world on horses both sleek and fast, flying across the heavens like stars glittering in the dark velvety sky, singing and laughing at their joyous flight and fancy. These magnificent beings are also known to move their homes on these same dates, and so to avoid disaster, they should never be disturbed for any reason.

The Trooping Faeries are the royals of the Faery world. A king and queen govern their societies and hold court four times a year, after which they and all the other Faeries ride forth in formal procession through the veil and into our surface world just for the joy of it. It's always an exciting and much looked forward to event for all and is met with great fanfare.

Beltaine Night, 2004

On a fortuitous Beltaine night in 2004, the Trooping Faeries made an unexpected visit into the forest by my home while my two friends and I naively sought their invisible portal. They raced down to earth from their lofty pathway and merrily rode nearby for a while. Though we didn't get to speak with them, it was an extraordinary evening for witnessing the mystery of it all. Afterwards, I sent out this prayer to those I'd wished to see:

> The path is wide,
> oh Ancient Ones,
> but the doorway narrows
> to the lands beyond time where you dwell.
> Open to me, bright Faery queen,
> and allow me entry,
> for my yearning heart beats as one with thee.

If you allow your own heart to soften and beat for the Faery beings and if your heart is pure, they may someday contact you, but don't be surprised if your encounter doesn't come about in quite the way you first planned. Faeries can be sly and full of mischief when they choose! So just relax and breathe deeply of the enchantment offered, for you'll find that where the Faeries are, there also lies the magic...

The narrow path through the oaks wound down towards a much wider path that veered off in both directions, left and right. A round cantaloupe moon hung above us and sent a pale orange light filtering through the tree branches making them appear like bent bony fingers reaching out in the dark of the night towards us.

As my two companions and I moved deeper into the grove, I suddenly seemed to see more clearly. Either the moon was rising higher in the night sky and providing us with more visibility, or I was getting used to the dark.

We turned off towards the right hand path, intent on walking the whole forest circle and resolved to test our individual courage and sense of adventure for finding the Faery doorway. I was more seasoned at this edge of consciousness, but my companions had just started their path through this world. Thus, I tried to take them slowly and cautiously to this point, but their youth and daring screamed in their heads to abandon that caution and run towards possible danger with arms wide open and adrenaline pumping.

While we continued on, I pulled in the energy, letting it surround us about six feet. All the while, I was silently listening, straining my ears for any noise indicating company. All I heard was the night sounds of an owl in a distant tree and the screech and chirp that comes from unseen bats, black against the black of the sky.

Round the circle we walked, slow, but with purpose. We talked of the challenges encountered through life and how we can use these challenges in a positive way to give us direction and a strong sense of self through our life path. We had looked to this evening for just such an instance, for it was Beltaine, a night when the veil between the worlds of Faery and human is thin and waiting to be penetrated by those seeking—or maybe not—that which sets these encounters in motion.

A noise to our right stopped us short, and we strained to recognize what it was. It was difficult to tell which direction it really came from because the night always seems to distort sound—like when you're in a cave and someone kicks a pebble, and the noise vibrates and bounces around back and forth off the walls. But the sound was just an instant, and then the silence stretched out before us like fog hanging eerily in the air.

Gathering our scattered energy back to us, we moved on quieter than before, for our resolve of discovery was growing weaker with every step. Giant redwoods loomed up on our left when we turned the bend in the pathway and passed two, then four, all the while plodding along in the dark with our path lit only by the orange moon.

We heard a strange and unexpected sound moving toward us, and then another, coming in soft, fast pats like raindrops hitting the tree branches from above then bouncing along the ground. I heard a sharp intake of breath, only to realize a second later that it was my own reaction to the unrecognizable noise.

If I could have described the sound in logical terms, I'd have said that intermittent rain was falling—and following us—along the path with some moving off to our right into the trees circling around us, except there hadn't been a cloud in sight all day. It had been quite clear and hadn't changed this evening. The sound was louder and heavier than raindrops, almost like horses' hooves trotting along in a group, muffled on a moss-covered path. First it came from the treetops, and then it shifted closer to us on the ground as it picked up speed.

My companions seemed to regress in age. No longer were they the invincible daring youths of twenty but now bordered more along the ages of nine or ten. They were throwing questions in my direction faster than I had time to think and answer, but by this point, I wasn't sure I had any tangible answers. This certainly wasn't something that I had ever passed through before, for my Faery allies usually eased in quietly and let me know in a familiar way that I was in their presence. What I felt from this experience was that this wasn't the ideal night to be where we were, and it was best to just head for home because we were totally unprepared for what we had sought. I stated such to my companions, and they heartily agreed.

We didn't meander slowly back along the pathway but made a hasty exit through the dark oaks towards the opening in the forest. I knew we were safe enough, for we had asked and were sent protection on our night's journey, but I was definitely relieved when we rounded the corner and stepped through the fencing and back onto the familiar road.

The glow of the street lamps erased the shadows and darkness of the forest as we realized our luck, for luck it was. Not all Otherworldly beings are friendly, and it was probably good we got out when we did. Also, we were lucky that we had the experience in the first place, for it turned out to be an encounter like we'd previously spoken of—one that brings with it the challenge of finding what we could use to gain a stronger sense of direction and purpose. We gave our thanks for it and vowed to get together again—only this time on a night that wasn't quite so open to the Hidden People riding through the veiled door.

Kiss The Wind

CHAPTER 7
Orb Faeries or Will-O'-the-Wisps

There has been a lot of speculation about orbs lately. They're more popular now that digital cameras have come into vogue and heightened their visibility, but there's also evidence of them on old 35mm prints from the last century, so even though they might have been ignored back then, they were still present. Maybe the answer to the influx of orb sightings lies in the fact that we're opening up to other forms of life and vibrations. The scales that have long obscured our sight are starting to fall off, or maybe the Otherworld is bleeding through into our own, and we are finally acknowledging its reality. Maybe it's just that now we can feel safe talking about it. The years of fearing such matters are slowly diminishing. Whatever the reason, let's take a look at some general ideas about orbs for they are here witnessing to us that they're going to stay.

Orbs are forms of energy that can react to people and places both indoors and out. They appear as bright white or blue lights that float in the air and are believed to be of a spiritual nature. In places where the energy is strong, they're particularly apparent, like where groups of people are gathered, holy sites, reportedly haunted places, or areas where trauma has been experienced.

Science considers orbs to be a natural energy structure that's always been part of our physical world but not readily seen until recently because we now have the ways and means to do so. Of course, this doesn't take into account those who've experienced them first hand but never discussed them openly.

Theories and beliefs abound concerning orbs. Some say orbs are souls of the departed who haven't passed on to the other side because of unfinished business; others believe that orbs are an ancient lineage of Faery beings called Will-O'-the-Wisps, who were not willing to reveal themselves again until humans were able to understand and assimilate the information. The latter believe that humankind's disconnection from the earth and lack of belief in the Faeries themselves has contributed to this long standing issue. Will-O'-the-Wisps are thought to be bog and water Faeries who appear as balls of light, which are mostly seen floating near water or marshy ground. Some say that they carry lanterns to guide travelers safely home. In parts of Europe, they are called Earthlights and are often seen hovering over tombs and burial mounds at night.

What I know of orbs is that they're very potent forms of energy that vibrate at higher levels than our physical world vibration. The lighter more ethereal orbs are departed spirits, our ancestral dead, while the denser more illuminated ones are the Fae. An old name for the Faery race is The Shining Ones or The Illuminated Ones because they were recognized as being of a shimmering brilliant light that was beyond the common effects of ordinary light, for it was a mystical light that came forth from the Otherworld where everything is part of this brilliant energy source. We see the ancestors and the Faeries as balls of light because it's the easiest form for them to assume in our third dimension—the less energy expended, the less energy it takes to maintain that form. The human spirit can and does take on its own form when necessary for specific reasons. Faery beings were created in conjunction with the earth and are the ones who animate and maintain it, so they can take on any form they choose because they live in the third and fourth dimensions simultaneously. Since humans are of a lower vibration, it's harder for us to see them though they have no trouble seeing us and find us pretty amusing stumbling around as we do.

The Fae can and do enter human evolution at times through the means of mating, or marriage and begetting children and what is called merging. When the Faery beings merge with humans, they change the energy structure of the humans, thus enabling them to draw themselves into human incarnation. The reason for this is to help humanity evolve to a higher consciousness by opening up their third-eye and allowing them to see the spirit realms and the divine nature of creation directly. Over time and with lack of use, the human third-eye slowly closed and disappeared until it's now considered to be the pineal gland that lies just outside the four cavities of the brain. Mystics believe the pineal gland to be the organ of the psychic mind. Only the Fae with the strongest wills consciously agree to merge with humans because it's hard for them to live in a human body that's of a lower vibration, for they are then permanently confined in a time and space not of their own. Thus they're unable to function normally.

The Faery races are one-element beings and humans are four, plus the life-force, so a human merged with a Faery can benefit by having their weakest element strengthened by the vitality of the Faery being's element. Thus they become stronger, more balanced, and able to comprehend and incorporate forgotten spiritual knowledge.

Sometimes Faery and human merging comes about through mutual agreement. Sometimes a misplaced penetration into other dimensions during human sexual union causes a magnetic pull, and then a Faery being is accidentally sucked into the stream of human incarnation at conception. In Dion Fortune's book *Psychic Self-Defense,* she calls this a psychic vortex, a funnel-shaped swirling that ascends into the other dimensions but sometimes gets deflected out of the human sphere of evolution—thus causing another type of being to incarnate into a human body. This transition can be very hard on Faeries because they will retain their memories of the world from whence they came. This split existence is often called "walking between the worlds" or "living with one foot on either side of the river" because they are neither totally here nor totally there; instead, they live half-way between this world and their own, so it's difficult for them to be fully committed to either.

For humans, the agreement and merging is often only remembered on a subconscious level—at least until the time when they have evolved enough to understand and handle the implications of what being part Fae, part human entails. A choice like this can be very trying because most will go through their lives feeling different and outside what is viewed as the normal routines of being human, thus setting them apart in a confusing way.

For Faeries, this merging can be beneficial by allowing them to balance the four energy patterns gained from humans they merge with, thus helping them learn more about how humanity thinks and functions on an emotional and physical level. Eventually, they will share this knowledge with other Elementals for their own evolution.

Many myths and legends revolve around human and Faery matings and marriages, the outcome being children born with both Fae and human blood. In the Norse, Icelandic, Germanic, Celtic, and Scandinavian myths, stories about humans with Faery ancestry are very commonplace. In Ireland, Conaire, the Irish high king of Tara was half Fae, half human, for it's told how his mother, Meas Buacchalla, was from the Otherworld and his father, Eterscele, was a human king in this world.

W.B. Yeats book, *The Celtic Twilight* relates a story of how the queen of Faery confirmed to a seer that some of them are born into mortal life, but it was unlawful to reveal who they were. The reason for this is because it would break the trust and agreement made between the mortal and Faery beings, thus causing unnecessary harm or danger to befall those concerned. It might be a little like discovering a UFO in your backyard. Fear of the unknown could take over, resulting in a modern day "witch hunt," so some things are just best kept quiet.

The attributes belonging to non-humans are listed here and in the Appendix for referral later. It's good to remember that not every hybrid will display each of these characteristics, for we are all unique, each in our own way/s.

Non-human and Human/Faery Hybrids:
Attributes and Characteristics

1)   Naturally gifted in the arts, such as music, storytelling, painting, writing, sculpture, etc.;

2)   Special "glow" or "shine" coming from within, like an inner light;

3)   Keen sense of humor, childlike enthusiasm, sense of fun, full of good-natured mischief but can be quiet and retiring also;

4)   Humans naturally drawn to them though they can't understand or explain why;

5)   Profound knowledge of all different areas of life and existence;

6)   Challenged to live within the confines of time schedules and what would be seen as the "normal" everyday routines of life;

7)   Spend a good deal of time in nature, either within their own yards and gardens or out in the wild places;

8)   Distinctly male and female but don't always identify themselves as being a certain sex, for they have a natural balance of male and female energies and are fully themselves in that balance;

9)   Generally neutral and objective;

10)   Curious, appear eccentric at times and follow their own instincts and inner perceptions throughout their lives rather than adhering to what society dictates;

11)   Found by humans to be odd, puzzling, mysterious, and/or aloof;

12)   Heightened sensory perception beyond the five senses and ability to sense things far before anyone else can;

13) Profound need for quietness and solitude—often perceived as lonely but aren't because they are constantly connected with the Otherworld;

14) Appear to carry a deep unexplainable sadness at times;

15) Look younger and age more slowly than most other humans;

16) Often feel out of place in the mundane world where others live comfortably—a sense of being dislocated or in the wrong time and place; strong distrust of humans and unwillingness to reveal themselves unless a long and abiding friendship has been established—sometimes never;

17) Ethereal beauty and charm that cannot be defined, depending on the caste they come from. Striking and unusual eyes, either in shape, color, or depth of soul;

18) Tend to shy away from technology and don't relate much to things that take them away from their natural connections with the world of nature, desiring instead to live more in the old ways—though if no other choice is given, they adapt very well to what is required;

19) Avoid large crowds and human physical contact as much as possible—unless it is with a mate, which they do not require but make as a conscious choice to learning;

20) Restless and longing for something they can't quite place;

21) Hard time dealing with human emotions and knowing how to handle them because in the land of Faery, emotions do not exist in the same way. They come into the human world to learn, and in turn, humans can learn from them if allowed;

22) Natural code of honor that is beyond most human understanding or ability to adhere to;

23) Often accused of being without natural affection or morals because human laws and Faery laws differ considerably

and the Faery, though in a human body, doesn't see anything wrong, for they live by the instincts which are inherent to them;

24)   Cartilage extension of the upper ear edge can have a slight crease or angle to it. Science has named this ear peak Darwin's Peak after Charles Darwin. They say it's an evolutionary leftover of the pointed mammal ear, but it's more frequently a sign of a non-human embodiment. Also, slightly rounded sloping fingernails;

25)   Can have acute allergies and intolerances to food and certain metal alloys, such as brass, steel, or iron. For some, piercings of any sort is out of the question because their bodies can react badly to them.

I imagine most people know or have met a non-human at one time but didn't realize it. Even the non-humans may not know it yet because as previously stated, they would have to be able to understand the implications and accept the responsibilities. For some, that can take a whole lifetime, for it's a matter of taking steps to know themselves like we all do, which is part of being a well-rounded individual.

There are places on the earth considered special magical haunts of the Elves and Faeries by modern and ancient peoples alike. Some of those are near water sources, like streams, springs, and seas, for water was considered a "betwixt and between" place that was neither completely in our physical world nor in the spiritual realm either because it was a portal into the Otherworld.

In the Netherlands where nearly half of the landmass has been reclaimed from the sea, there are many places where Faeries reside. The rivers Rhine, Waal, and Meuse are the country's main distributaries, and the North Sea lies to the north and west, which makes this a land where water is the ruler. Flooding is a constant danger, and the extensive system of dikes, dams, and sand dunes are relied upon to protect it. It's also a country where part of my racial heritage comes from.

Because of this, my family's long time penchant for settling near water was fixed hundreds of years ago and came naturally to us.

The following first person account is my father's experience of an encounter that happened when he was fourteen. It occurred at one of those watery in-between spots in Northern California and partly explains how our family came to be so independent, restless, and, well, different.

An Encounter with Three Orbs

Long ago—and a long time it was, indeed—a little creek meandered off from a great river that flowed out of the foothills. A green patchy tract of land lay between them both, and we knew that in winter this area was flooded until spring, but summer was high now and the waters had receded, so this is where we settled until fall when the rains came again. It was a wild country, full of things seen, unseen, and some things most city folks didn't want to know about—a country where magic quietly floated in the air and mingled with our lives. Considering that our family let their inherent instincts lead them—those deepest instincts for being in tune with the natural world and living according to her rhythms instead of battling against them—these sorts of things didn't faze us much, for we took what came with a grain of salt, which is an asset that living off the land can bring.

I was the sixth child of eight, born into a family with great strength of character, determination, and resourcefulness, plus a lot of minding our own business thrown in the mix, for that was just the way of it. On this morning I awoke with a flash of light flickering through the trees against my closed eyelids, so I rolled over and tried to go back to sleep, but it was useless. I needed to get up. Even with fresh hay underneath me and the soft humming of bees in the nearby clover willing me to let go and dream, I had more important things to do, for the day was just beginning, and it was my turn to rustle up breakfast. At that moment, though, what I really wanted to do was just lie there, watching the bees drone lazily in the morning sun and listen to my mother rattle pans around in the makeshift kitchen of the two-room hut we'd acquired for the summer. It was an old ramshackled thing that sat three feet off the ground supported by cement blocks and wooden legs with no interior walls, just lap siding on the exterior and a thin sheet of metal for the roof, but it was shelter for a while and would do.

I kicked off my blanket, yawned, and stretched. My younger brother was dragging a bucket across the yard towards the creek for water, and he struggled while pulling it along, which scattered our six chickens and stirred up a cloud of dust that made me cough.

After reluctantly shaking off my sleepiness, I leaned down and grabbed my knife, fishing pole, and jute bag that we used for carrying home the fish we caught. Then I cut across the creek bank and walked down into a gully to gather green-husked black walnuts that local folk sometimes used for catching fish. I threw the walnuts into the bag and moved on towards my destination.

Walking alongside the river, I noticed the area where I usually fished had an oddly dark and foreign feel to it, which made me uneasy, so I headed towards an inlet down river instead. I stopped along the edge and tied the bag's top with string, then threw it in, only to find that within a short time some fish floated to the surface, so I grabbed the bag, pulled them out, baited my hook and tossed in the line.

While waiting for something to happen on the baited end of my pole, a breeze suddenly kicked up and hummed along like voices in the air, so I closed my eyes to listen, but instead it was the faint rush of wind that stirred the leaves in the trees and not the voices that I'd first thought. I was a little disappointed and half-inclined to grab the fish and go but found myself momentarily unable to move, for I felt strangely hypnotized by the very presence of something I couldn't see but that held me in place in spite of myself.

Time passed . . . and when my father finally found me, that time appeared to have vanished while I sat there oblivious to the world. Two hours were mysteriously gone. Where they went, I couldn't say, but I was left with bits and pieces of strange memories whirling around in my fourteen-year-old brain that I knew weren't mine but didn't know where they came from.

I didn't understand what had happened nor could I explain to my father the vacant look on my face when he found me. All I could do was tell him I was alright and slowly follow him back home.

The remainder of the day was a blur, and as day passed to dusk, I was feeling more and more apprehensive about the coming night. I knew that something inevitable was moving my way, but I wasn't sure what it might be. My family had questioned me earlier about the incident by the river, and I'd told them what I remembered, but none of it really made sense to us, so in the end, they left me alone because they figured I was fine.

Later that night as I sat by the fire with one of my older brothers, he asked me again what had happened, figuring now that we were alone, I would talk more freely.

"What in the name of all we hold dear went on out there, really? I know what you've said, but I don't buy it. You don't scare easy, and when father brought you back, you looked like you'd seen some unearthly spirit, so I know there's something you're not saying. What is it?"

I looked at him long and hard, trying to recall everything I had felt: the breathless stirring of the air, the sound of voices, the feeling of a presence beside me, the loss of time. It still made no sense to me, and I was confused by the whole ordeal.

"Look, I really can't explain any better to you than I did to anyone else what happened. All I know is that there was a breeze, and then suddenly the air got thin and quiet, and some sort of silvery sparkles seemed to dance around in the shadows of the trees across the river, and I felt like someone was standing beside me, watching."

"Though I'm still kind of foggy and unsure, the presence felt almost female, but that could have just been my imagination because I can't quite figure out what I really felt. I've told father the same thing, which is that I lost track of time, and basically that's what happened. Otherwise, I don't know what to say, but you're right. I was scared."

He scratched his head, ruffling his hair into a tangle and said, "You remember that guy Jim we met last year on the road, the one that camped with us a few days? He told me once when we were out hunting that while he was visiting with his sister a few months before, she'd gone washing in the nearby creek and was gone a long time, so everyone went to look for her, but she was nowhere to be found. After a few hours of searching, they finally stumbled upon her wandering a mile from where she was supposed to be. He said she had the strangest vacant expression on her face, and they weren't sure what to do for her, so they wrapped her in warm blankets and gave her something to eat, and eventually she snapped out of it, but after that she took to staring off into the distance now and then like she was searching for something. It sounds like you might have had a similar experience."

"Well, maybe. Maybe not," I said. "But I have this lingering feeling that won't go away, like I've been touched by something, and if I take just one step, it will all be made perfectly clear because it's already familiar to me in some unexplainable way. When I was looking across the river, I couldn't really see anything in detail, but I knew what was over there as clearly as if I was standing in that spot, and all I'd have to do is think it, and I'd be able to be there instantly, but I couldn't move. That's the whole point. It was strange! Honestly though, it's giving me chills, so I don't really want to think about it anymore tonight. I just want to forget it for now, ok? Let's not talk about it anymore."

He looked at me rather worriedly, then stood up, and said, "Sure, sure, I understand. Why don't you get some sleep? You'll probably feel better in the morning anyway. Goodnight."

After everyone was in bed asleep, I got up and stirred the remaining coals of the fire into a pile with a stick and watched the end of it blaze red with heat. Shadows appeared in the burning coals, and I leaned forward to watch their movements. The rising sparks from the fire danced and crackled in the air, and the wind suddenly kicked up. It was then I knew they were coming, and I also knew there was nothing I could do about it but wait, and so I waited.

I don't remember how much time passed, but I do remember what happened . . .

Behind me I thought I heard a sound, so I turned and in the half-light of the fire, I saw three round balls of soft blue light floating in V-formation low to the ground towards me. The largest one in front was about eight inches in diameter, and the other two smaller ones in back hung on either side, spinning slowly as they moved. Suddenly the air stilled. Not a leaf stirred, the little creek was quiet, and I couldn't breathe. All there was was darkness, silence, and fear—which was almost intolerable—and I shook so hard my teeth rattled, but there was no strength in me to run. I sat quietly and continued to wait while the orbs moved towards me, slower now, and when they pressed close to my chest, I gave out a loud exhale of breath, and they entered my body, one after the other, and I felt the peculiar sensations of fire and ice, joy and sorrow, the pains of a hard death and the exhilaration of new life, and a longing in my soul so cruel as to make me cry out and ache for a place I did not remember. Then darkness took me down to sleep.

In the morning when I woke, my head was clear and my vision sharp. My senses seemed somewhat heightened, and I puzzled over this but then let it go. The days continued much the same afterwards, the comings and goings of a normal life, but each night for the next two nights, they came again, and I both burned and froze though I did not fight. On the fourth night they ceased to come, and I was relieved but I was also somewhat saddened, for I felt akin to them in some strange way, like we were connected in a manner I did not recognize or understand.

Then the years came and went, both a passing of time and a passing of lives, melting away into a long line of existence as I married, had a family, and watched as each new generation displayed some unique gift of heightened awareness and unnatural good luck. Am I now able to explain what happened in a way that folks would understand and believe? No, I cannot, for it's not in my power to do so, but I can say that the experience made a believer out of me in the lives and intelligences of beings other than our own.

Now I am old, though older than I appear, and I've learned through the years that people of land and water, as we were, will live their lives quietly with a gentle tolerance of what may come, for some things are often not what they appear to be, as we ourselves learned.

So our lives ebbed and flowed like the waters we lived beside, for we were born of water—water was our life—and back to the water we shall eventually return to manifest our dreams and visions in the lucid primordial sea, always bound to it like we are now bound to the great mystery of that experience, forever woven into the tapestry of our lives, spinning there still where it began so long ago.

Kiss The Wind

CHAPTER 8
Water Faeries

For this chapter I've slightly revised the story of the wandering sea that I was told as a child. It's a tale about the Faeries and the sacred aspect of water, for the sea is the womb of the Goddess where life originally began and still the abode of many an ancient sea god and water Faery.

Water was sacred to many cultures, but to the Celts it was the blood of the Goddess herself, for the water that flowed through the earth was directly related to the life-force energy that fed the land and kept it vibrant and alive for the inhabitants living there.

Water was also the venue for attaining wisdom and knowledge. In Irish mythology the sacred well of Conla or the Well of Segais that feeds the River Boyne was where Brandan, the Salmon of Wisdom, lived. Nine hazel trees grew around the well, and it was the hazelnuts from the wisdom trees that fed the salmon of the pool and rendered him wise. Drinking water from the well of wisdom—the well of inspiration—would open inner vision, and the source of all knowledge would flow into that person.

Getting to the Otherworld or the Faery realm was always accomplished by crossing over water. The 14th century Scottish ballad of Thomas the Rhymer, or True Thomas as he later became known, tells us that while Thomas sat by a flowering hawthorn tree, he met and was taken into the land of Faery for seven years by the Elfland queen herself. On their travels, they passed over many rivers connecting the two worlds until eventually wading through a river of blood that was referred to by the Faery queen as "the blood that's shed on earth" or "the blood of our ancestors."

At the death of the physical body, we all go back to become part of the earth, eventually mingling with the waters flowing through the planet and making us our own forebears in a sense. Through this blending process, we are both genetically our own lineage and also of those not our direct bloodline, and so we can access the knowledge they, themselves, bore. Water, the gateway to Faery, has long been associated with the gift of dreaming, cleansing, and healing, for the sacred living waters of the land flow up from the invisible underground realms where these ancient gifts manifest.

At the last battle of Camlan, the Welsh hero, King Arthur, was taken to the Otherworld—what the poets called Avalon—across a magical unnamed lake that bordered the two worlds. Morgan le Fay (Morgan the Faery queen), Nimue (the Lady of the Lake), and two Otherworld Fae women ferried him over to be cured of the wounds he received in the battle.

Avalon is the magical Otherworld Island known as "Eamhain Abhlach," the land of apples, where the priestess of the Great Mother Goddess lived and carried on her traditions. It's the enchanted lands across the water into Faery where Arthur awaits his return home.

Water can be used as a focal point for meditation when seeking to understand your inner self or your life-path. Water moves things along and clears the blockages that build up over each lifetime, providing a clear understanding of how to work through personal issues, for water is associated with our unconscious emotions and the repressed fears we often choose not to see.

There are many Faery beings associated with water besides the Elemental Undines: The Kelpie, Naiad, Selkie, Rusalky, Nixie, Asari and Gwagged Annwn are just a few, not to mention the Loch Ness Water Horse, which is considered Fae by some. But whichever Faery you encounter or body of water you cross, perhaps luck will smile on you, and the Old Ones of the mounds and seas will take you to the halls of song and mirth if you reverently seek the doorways into the deep places by honoring water as the vast magical portal that it is. It's a place

where ancient memory still runs parallel with
come twilight climb a hill that weaves into the *
the earth or take a coracle into the heart of a lak
cuts the thread to what binds you to physical reality. *
you might find you'll never be quite the same again.

The Tale of a Wandering Sea

Water is a mystery, a portal to the past, a doorway to the
Otherworld. Strange tales have been told of a wandering sea
and the night she slipped her sandy banks to tread the paths
through the lands of Faery. Many a Faery child has been put to
bed by stories of how the surface-world sea got lost in the
mists and appeared in their own time and space, exhausted
with-searching for her home.

Finally, the boundless light of that mysterious Otherworld's
moon rocked the lost sea to sleep in its luminous silvery arms,
for there in the light and silence of that perfect moon laid the
power to give to the wanderer. Long she slept, that curious sea,
and a kinship was formed between her and the moon while in
that deep and intoxicating slumber.

When upon waking from the moon's soft embrace, the sea
found herself no longer to be any ordinary bit of water but part
of a large, ancient lineage of primordial sea-gods whose lives
ruled the Elemental forces upon the surface-world, though they
dwelt in the light of the Other. For their moon was the giver of
physical form when it rested upon the surface-world sea, and
out of the Otherworld came the spark to animate what would
someday become the world of matter.

And it is still told round the fires and hearths how the
wandering sea got lost in the mists and found her purpose in
the arms of the moon and the lands of the "Others" of Faery.

Kiss The Wind

CHAPTER 9
Elves

Everyone dreams, but not everyone remembers them. Dreams that are easily remembered usually occur right before waking, and if not written down immediately, they'll start to fade. The best way to learn from dreams is to keep pen and paper at our bedside and record them the moment we awake up.

Swiss psychologist Carl Jung believed that dreams are an expression of the collective unconscious, the part of the inborn human mind that shares universal knowledge and offers guidance and insights into our inner life and who we are innately. Dreams enable us to overcome fears and problems, create and accomplish goals, cure illness, and view life in happy new ways. By regarding our dreams as important tools for wisdom and self-change, we can create a stronger, more balanced life, for through the symbols and metaphors of dreams, we come to know our true selves.

Many cultures used dreams as ways to foretell the future and access different levels of reality and different dimensions. The Australian Aborigines have a psychic realm similar to the collective unconscious called the Dreamtime that resembles the Celtic Otherworld or the land of the inner workings of humanity. More value was put on the dreams of these cultures than they are today, for the tribal Dreamwalker was highly honored as someone who could dream on behalf of the whole tribe and speak with the spirits of the departed or communicate with their deities to find answers to questions concerning the people.

Dreams aren't viewed in the same way in society today; instead, they are undervalued and viewed as nothing more than Flights of Fancy. We're told by scientists that we need to dream because dreaming helps us relax, release pent-up stress, and keep our minds functioning normally.

Dreams can take us into the world of Faery, a world that is just as real as ours only more in alignment with the inner workings of nature but more pure and unspoiled by human greed and corruption.

Whether we use dreams for self-exploration or gaining entry into Faeland, what we experience in their world can help increase our understanding of our own nature, as well as all of humanity by reconnecting to the land and to each other, thus eliminating our sense of alienation from both of them. If we use and honor the ability to transcend physical reality through the dreamtime to work with the beings of this other consciousness, we can begin to make strides towards bringing wholeness to a planet and people so in need of healing.

In Chapter 12 you'll find a more definitive guide to the personalities of the Elves, so for a deeper understanding and more information on them, read on, dear friends.

One of my own experiences with the Elven race happened while dreaming, and it went something like this.

Journey Through the Dreamtime

The flat smooth amethyst I'd placed under my pillow was going to help me journey to the Otherworld tonight, for I knew that amethysts protected travelers, induced dreams, increased spiritual awareness of other dimensions, and helped open the psychic center. Amethysts are positive stones that hold all those powers, and I'd planned on accessing them. I felt completely safe about taking the amethyst with me because it was going to aid in my traveling the roads and pathways of Faery tonight, for I wanted to acquire more knowledge of that realm. Dreamtime was my way of doing it, so I flipped off the bedroom light and moved to the other side of the bed where I slipped in, snuggling up into my covers, and sliding my hand carefully under my pillow to check on the stone.

I was going over the day's events in my head and thinking about the things I'd accomplished when I realized I was standing outside in my backyard looking at my neighbor's fence. Beams of light were peaking around the corners of his red brick chimney as the sun was slowly sinking, which made me appreciate how pretty it looked with the sun playing hide-and-go-seek. The aroma of freshly baked cookies drifted seductively down the street towards me, and I knew that someone in the neighborhood was baking.

As I stood under my kitchen window sniffing, I noticed two men walk out from around the corner of my garden where I have an altar of small standing stones set up. When I'd moved here, the pie-shaped area was nothing but an empty piece of ground filled with holes and junk that needed to be taken to the dump. Over the years I'd carefully cleared it out and fixed it up, dedicating it to the Goddess and all the Otherworld beings that wished to occupy it.

As these two men walked in single file across my yard, I took note of them. The taller one in front had dark brown hair that waved around the collar of his knee-length cape, and the one behind had hair the color of pale moonlight. They wore pants made from some kind of homespun silken cloth, their feet were bare, and they were dressed in exactly the same green and brown shades. Other than their hair color, they were almost like mirror images of each other.

They seemed to take no note of me, however, for they were both stepping lightly across my yard and looking towards my neighbor's house when suddenly the taller one turned his head, looked directly at me and smiled as though not surprised that I was there watching. His face was attractive, friendly, and seemed to light up when he smiled, like it was glowing from the inside. I suddenly felt a curious need to talk to him but couldn't find my tongue and wasn't sure what to say if I did, so instead I decided to let it go.

It feels rather odd having two men wandering across my backyard and coming from a place with only one access, but there they are, and what can I do about it anyway? I thought.

But wait a minute. No one dresses in such a fine earthy way any longer, and no one is as beautiful or light of foot as these two are, so they must be Elves, not men! I thought.

Then the Elf facing me nodded, and I started to step towards them but realized that a second ago, I'd been in my bed thinking . . . and in the very next moment that's exactly where I found myself—still lying in bed like I'd never left.

I was certainly disappointed to come back right then, for how often do you discover Elves in your backyard, but my conscious thoughts had moved me home before I was ready to go.

Apparently the amethyst worked better and faster than I expected. I'd wanted to travel, and travel I did though not very far, for it appeared that my backyard was the perfect place for an Elven encounter. I was glad I'd put the time and energy into making it beautiful because they seemed to be very comfortable there, and I was pleased to have them acknowledge this by a visit.

Chapter10
The Sidhe: Council of Nine

The Sidhe are the ancient gods of Irish mythology called the Túatha Dé Danann, the People of the Goddess Danu, and sometimes referred to as the Shining Ones. The Túatha, as they are frequently called, arrived in Ireland from a place told to be beyond the North Wind on the first of May, or Beltaine, bringing with them all their expertise in magic, as well as their artistic abilities and scientific knowledge, which some suggest were employed in creating and raising the stone circles and seasonal observatories that are scattered around the countryside and believed to be the places where they dwell.

A race known as the Fir Bog was already entrenched in Ireland when these newcomers arrived, so the Túatha fought them for possession of the land. After winning the battle, they proceeded to clear it, which caused new rivers and lakes to spring up, thus testifying to their intrinsic right to occupy Ireland. But this right was eventually superseded by a race calling themselves the Milesians, or the Sons of Mil who are the ancestors of the present day Gaels.

Upon the arrival of the Milesians, they and the Túatha battled, and the People of the Goddess Danu retreated into the earth to live in the hills, mounds, and cairns, or those places that are otherwise called the sidhe mounds of the hollow hills, or the realms of the Otherworld.

Sidhe folk are now considered the Faery race, but they are not the diminutive sprites that live in your garden. Instead, they are a race that is great in stature and power, being wise, immortal and demanding honor, respect, and restitution for the ongoing abuse of the land, for they are the guardians and caretakers of the earth. It is they who maintain its balance and fertility, they who grant the right for the continuation of a species, and they who make the final decision to the outcome of our world.

Could the council featured in the following story be nine of the Sidhe, great leaders and archetypes who hold the powers that affect us all? Here is a list of the possible candidates:

- Aengus or Aonghus is associated with the passage of time. Legend says that when Aengus was conceived, his mother Boinn was put under an enchantment so that the passing of the nine month gestation period only seemed like one day—hence, his link with time. Aengus is a god of love but also of trickery that is never malicious or harmful since it comes in the form of practical jokes to lighten up an otherwise tense or stressful situation.

- Boann or Boinn is a very ancient goddess who gave her name to the Boyne River in Ireland. She is associated with fertility and the inspiration of the Divine. She is a goddess of creation.

- Bridgit or Brighid is a goddess of poetry, smithcraft, and healing and is associated with the guardianship and protection of the land and the well-being of domesticated animals.

- Dagda, or Daghda is recognized as one of the first of the "parent" gods, or the father/chief of the Irish pantheon of god-beings. He is associated with the basic earthly functions of eating, drinking, and sexuality. He has a harp that has the power to call forth the seasons. He is also associated with the fertility of the land and with agriculture.

- Dian Ceacht is a god of the healing arts of the physical body and of reincarnation. He helps provide a way to return from the Otherworld once the portal has been passed.

- Lugh is a god of prophecy, beauty and healing. He is associated with knowledge of both the dark and light sides of existence and working with those opposing sides to achieve a balanced lifestyle.

- Midir or Midhir is the god of the Underworld or the Otherworld realm. He is master of illusion, enchantment, and deception, as it sometimes is in the Faery realm, for in the land of Faery things are not always what they seem.

- Morrigan or Mor-Rioghain is a war goddess. She is associated with death, grief, war, and shape-shifting. She is said to have uttered a prophecy, detailing the fate of the world and its inhabitants in their final days.

- Ogma or Ogham is credited with the development of the Ogma script, an alphabet containing twenty-five letters in the form of a straight line bisecting a longer line or stave. The Ogma was used by the bards of Ireland and Britain to secretly pass on information and knowledge to others in their Druid sect. He is associated with the eloquence of speech, poetic inspiration, learning and letters. He is also the god of the physical skills of a champion.

Significance of Nine

The number nine was a significant and powerful number throughout the ancient traditions of our ancestors because it was always seen as sacred, carrying aspects of the Divine Power. The Hebrews referred to the number nine as the symbol of immutable Truth and Pure Intelligence because it produces itself when multiplied.

Celtic legend symbolized the number nine as a central number with eight directions on a compass and the center point equaling nine. There were nine worlds in the Celtic universe and the Triple-Goddess—maiden, mother, and crone—are thrice three, for each is an aspect that ends up equaling nine.

For the Celtic festival of Midsummer, it was always custom to throw nine different kinds of herbs on the celebratory fire for luck and continuing fertility: St John's Wort, Rue, Vervain, Mistletoe, Lavender, Feverfew, Meadowsweet, Heartsease, and either Oxalis, Clover, or Shamrock.

Nine woods were required for the starting of the central bonfire in the celebration of Beltaine, and it was attended by eighty-one men (eight plus one equals nine), nine at a time, which is nine times nine equaling eighty-one and then reducing back to nine.

Numerology tells us that the number nine is the greatest of all numbers with the energy of the previous numbers infused into it. It represents the completion of tasks, endings, transitions, and the ability to promote improvement on a global level. Perfection, intuition, artistic endeavors, and universal oneness are energized by the number nine. Its process is being able to understand the true value of life, love, and the greater good for humanity and the planet.

To the Norse seers of old, there were nine distinct aspects to each human. In addition, there were nine worlds sheltered by the cosmic tree Yggdrasil:

- Asgard, home of the Aesir gods;

- Vanaheim, home of the Vanir gods;

- Alfheim, home of the *light* Elves;

- Nidavellir, home of the dwarfs;

- Midgard, home of humankind;

- Jontunheim, home of the Giants;

- Svartalfheim, home of the *dark* Elves;

- Hel, home of the inglorious dead;

- Niflheim, the region of everlasting cold and endless night.

The Norse god Odin acquired wisdom and discovered the Runes through a self-inflicted ordeal by hanging himself on the World Tree for nine days and nine nights, pierced by a sword. This was considered a spiritual death induced for the betterment of the people by allowing him insight in which to release the Runes' full potential.

In Greece the number nine was the number of the nine daughters of Zeus and Mnemosyne who were the nine Goddesses that inspired the creation of literature and the arts. Mnemosyne and Zeus slept together for nine consecutive nights to create their daughters, the Muses. It's the Goddess Mnemosyne who is considered the supreme source of imagination, knowledge, and memory, of which the Muses are a part.

To the Egyptians, the council of nine was originally deities worshipped on the island of Atlantis, the legendary continent that was overwhelmed beneath the sea along with its inhabitants due to the Atlanteans' misuse of power. Later the council went to live in Egypt as part of the Heliopolis, the "City of the Sun," and was called "The Nine."

Modern pagans celebrate eight holy days or festivals that center on the earth's seasonal cycles with the center point, the ninth point, being spirit or Source. The eight festivals consist of the Winter Solstice, Imbolc, the Spring Equinox, Beltaine/Beltine, the Summer Solstice, Lughnassadh, the Autumn Equinox, and Samhain.

Even the Faery race is said to have nine ages to their existence. Alexander Carmichael tells us in his book *Carmina Gadelica* that they possess nine ages with nine times nine periods of time that make-up each age.

Horses and the Faeries

Horses are also an important aspect to this vision. The Faeries have a long affinity with horses, which were often the ones that would carry the Faery folk along the pathways that wound between their invisible world and the mundane world of mortals.

Faery horses are bred for their beauty, speed, and lofty spirits. They are often white in color, and their chests are muscular, their nostrils quivering with a restless excitement while their large flame-filled eyes show their strong and fiery inbred natures. A bush or tree is said to catch fire when they pass by because they are known to be so swift in their flight that an energetic friction follows in their wake. Though the average horse lives twenty-five to thirty years, the Faery steed is able to live far more than a hundred, which shows their fine breeding and magical powers.

In the Irish tale of Niamh and Oisin, Niamh of the Golden Head is the daughter of the high king of Faery who rules the Land of the Young, the sacred lands of the Otherworld. She had fallen in love with Oisin, who lived in the mortal physical world and was the son of the great warrior and guardian Finn of the Fianna. Niamh desired that Oisin should travel back to the land of Faery with her on the back of her powerful white horse to live as her husband and king. Oisin agreed, much to the sorrow of his father Finn and the warriors of the Fianna because Finn knew that the power of Faery was stronger than that of the mundane, and it would be the last time they would all be gathered together as one united branch of warriors. Oisin's love of the Faery maid Niamh overshadowed all else, and he could not resist going with her into the enchanted realms. So he mounted onto the back of her horse, and they rode off towards the sea where the Faery lands lie hidden over the horizon.

Chalk drawings of horses are inscribed into the lands of the British Isles with the White Horse of Uffington being the most recognized. Across the countryside, twenty-one of the most significant horse drawings are still maintained today, and it's these drawings that are carved into the hills. The connection between the denizens of Faery and the hills and mounds is apparent, for those mystical beings live within the hills, mounds, and raths of the lands, and the horse is sacred to them.

Symbolically, horses correspond to spiritual understanding and the ability to think and reason clearly on spiritual subjects, for the ancients accepted the horse as a representation of higher intelligence, which is still being honored today through esoteric practices. Like cats, horses are highly sensitive animals that respond to invisible presences only they can see, which is one reason they're associated with the physical and the spiritual realms. On the spiritual plane, shamans use horses to carry them to other realms of existence and to transverse gateways into the Otherworld.

It is from this other world that a new age and order is brought forth, and the black horse and rider in the following story were the messengers sent forth to facilitate this new age of wisdom, for creation and beginnings have always come out of the darkness of the womb of Source.

Metaphysically, the color black is the color of seriousness and authority, as well as being the bridge to the lands of the Otherworld where knowledge and the power to accomplish are manifested with the help of its established inhabitants: the gods, ancestors, and Faery beings. Black is the combination of all the colors of pigment and will generate and distribute heat when used in physical objects, which can then be utilized to cleanse, refine, and remove impurities.

The next story, which manifested in a vision, tells of the decision of the council to send the black rider so that the "seal" could be opened, and a new millennium would be ushered in. This new millennium would give humanity the opportunity to change their world consciousness by turning away from the self-destructive path of abusing power so as not to make that mistake again.

Will we heed the voices of the Old Ones and choose wisdom and life over ignorance and death? The wheels have been set in motion. As always, the choice is in our hands.

The Dark Rider

The man on the horse rode hard across the flat, barren landscape. My reality had collapsed, and everything was now two-dimensional. As I watched the rider's black silhouette against the sepia colored background, there were no details in this strange scene to help make up my usual perceptions of reality, just this fractured starkness of black on tan.

I watched him ride on, sitting as a man on a winged dragon riding the wind. I marveled at the swift and assured way his black horse kept on course, for this dark horseman did not let up in pursuit of his goal.

Faster and faster he rode towards his mission, galloping hard, then abruptly turning and heading in my direction. Six feet away he halted and appeared to stare down at me from astride his mount. Though I couldn't make out the details of his face, I felt his focus, which made me shiver, and I turned my head to keep hold of my fear.

Hanging in the air between us, a thin veil of lambskin parchment suddenly appeared with words written in a script I didn't know or recognize. As this horseman continued to watch me, I felt him reading my thoughts. Instead of just standing there in fear, I found the courage to turn my head and look back at him and challenge his authority, for I knew he was challenging mine.

While we assessed each other, an odd sulfurous odor rose in the air, and the vellum ignited in the center with brilliant flames of blue and then spread out to orange and consumed the veil from the inside out.

Through this fire and heat, the horseman made a silent announcement to me—from mind to mind—that the burning of the veil was meant to call forth a melting away of the fear, ignorance, and abuse of power that has kept the world blind and chained for thousands of years. An awakening of the human spiritual soul through a higher state of consciousness and a return to traditional truths would then be brought back after being ignored and then lost.

I sensed that this long awaited message to our world would open the door to a new reality and lay the foundation for the future evolution of humanity. Truth would then begin again in earnest.

On two separate evenings, this was the second vision I'd been sent. The first manifested three nights before and was the precursor to the coming of the rider in black. As I sat in bed thinking about the second vision that I just had of the rider, the first one slowly came back to me in its fullness, and I then relived the first night's vision . . .

Evening had brought a full moon, creeping over the thatched-roofed building, and that round moon was as perfectly symmetrical as the room in which I stood. From inside I could see that the ceiling was low and made from wooden beams a foot wide that anchored it to the walls for support. The building was fashioned from logs chinked with mud, and the window shutters were thrown open into the night, which allowed a cool breeze to wisp in and ruffle my hair.

The room smelled of the faint scent of sage and applewood. I guessed the scents were coming from a brazier fire alight behind a green silk curtain across the room because it glowed there, faintly green.

Dark had settled in deeply but for the fire's light, and I stood watching it dance on the silk, feeling the energy of someone in the room with me. I turned in anticipation to find a man standing against the far wall, waiting for me to acknowledge him.

I could see from the firelight he was a big man with a rugged but kind face that appeared darker in places where the light hid behind his bold features. He was dressed in gray cloth with a blue cloak thrown carelessly over his shoulders.

He stepped across the room towards me in three giant steps. A flash of copper reflected in my eyes off the clasp on his cloak. Then his big hand swung over and pulled back the green curtain as he said to me, "Look, all the Lords and High Chiefs are here for the meeting."

And I did look to find six men and three women, sitting around a large wooden table laid out with rolls of parchment and maps and writing material.

These nine were deep in conversation, so I shrank back behind the curtain to try to remain hidden. As I did, I made a mental note of their apparent royal status, for eight of them were regally dressed in scarlet, purple, and green trimmed robes. They wore gold and jewels on their hands and jeweled crowns upon their heads, but the ninth person was a man all in black, except for a round silver star brooch attached to his breast. As I watched him, the brooch suddenly grew bright and threw an intense white light across the room that burned into the far wall and made me shield my eyes momentarily.

When I looked up, he made eye contact with me over the rim of a silver goblet held in his hands. As he raised it to his lips and drank, I sensed he held some strength and power that was beyond my understanding but which I would soon learn.

Suddenly the crackling fire roared loudly, and my sight blurred, so I stepped back from the edge of the doorway and tripped over my own feet, caught myself, then staggered towards the door with the heady smell of sage now suffocating me. I stumbled out the door with my hands tingling and the excitement rushing to my head like it would burst through the top. I fell to my knees, speaking aloud my prayers for protection, and then I saw no more.

CHAPTER 11
House Brownies

Brownies are small, solitary house Faeries who are very good at hiding. They attach themselves to certain families but don't interact much personally once they're established. At night they aid in tasks around the house like cleaning, churning milk, finding lost items, and protecting the home from unpleasant spirits. They prevent accidents from happening while you're away from home on holiday because they'll carefully look after it, being one of the things they take as a serious responsibility.

They live in dark, confined places like cupboards, cellars, closets, attics, stairwells, and sometimes outdoors in caves and hollow trees.

They will abandon a house if the owners misuse them because they are painfully sensitive to ridicule and abuse. They don't like to be fussed over or mocked and will turn against you if you're too direct or critical, causing troubles like spoiling your food, making things you need disappear permanently, or bringing illness and accidents to the family of the house.

House Brownies don't like to be seen and will not speak to humans directly, for they don't like directness in any manner. They prefer to be left alone. They'll let you know they're living in your house when they get good and ready, usually by taking something and then eventually returning it to a place where you've obviously looked before but didn't see it.

Traditionally Brownies like to be fed milk, honey, cake, and ale in exchange for their help and hard work, but don't offend them by giving them clothes, or they'll be forced to leave— usually in a huff.

A house and family is chosen by a Brownie, not the other way around; however, if you want to make your home more conducive to brownie activity, start by being the kind of person a brownie would be attracted to: kind, honest, hardworking and non-intrusive. They also love harps, so playing harp music couldn't hurt.

It's said that in the 18th century, brownies traveled across the Atlantic Ocean with the Scottish immigrants, but since they—like all Faeries—can move through time and space at will, this is more of a fanciful thought than an actuality. Not that a Brownie wouldn't be happy stowing away in a large trunk of clothes or in the bow hold of a ship, but it's more likely they just manifested once their families got established in the New World.

House Brownies are small and hairy with large eyes, wrinkled faces, and flat noses. They sometimes wear old tattered brown clothes, but in most instances, they wear nothing at all. In the Highlands of Scotland they're said to have no fingers or toes, just flat palmed hands that work just as well without them. Their Welsh cousins, the Bwca or Bwbach, are similar in appearance, except for their long noses.

The Brownies mostly go naked because of their all over hairy bodies. It is said they get their name from the brown clothes they wear, but this is highly unlikely since they don't normally wear clothing.

No one is really sure of the origins of Brownies, but they're found mostly in Cornwall, Scotland, Orkney, Shetland, and Northern England. Wherever their original beginnings were, they're now encountered on the American Continent. They seem to have taken quite a liking to this land because Americans are so unaware of Faeries and the history of Faery beliefs that the Brownies feel they can comfortably make their homes here and not be disturbed. If you enjoy the arrangement with your Brownie, just remember to leave a bowl of milk and honey out for them on occasion. Never offer them a suit of clothes or offend them by talking to them directly, and all will go smoothly for as long as you both choose. If you find that items in your house are suddenly starting to vanish unexplainably, then the best guess would be that you had a House Brownie move in. This is my own discovery of an unseen guest.

The Hall Closet

The green velvet was folded neatly in half and laid out across the cutting board on the floor. I was making an ankle-length cape, and the pattern was simple enough because it only had two pieces, the four paneled main body and the hood. This was the second cape I made from this pattern, so I expected it to go off without a hitch; little did I know that wasn't going to happen.

It was a month before my Samhain party, and I wanted my new cape to be a focal point. It was a costumed affair, and the requirements were to inspire the spirits to join us in the celebration by dressing in a way that they'd recognize and appreciate.

After the pattern was pinned on, I got my scissors and began to cut. The process was problem-free because the four panels were all cut at the same time and then the hood, so it went smoothly. Afterwards I put it all in the closet to wait for another day to start sewing. (A closet was the telling point in the end.)

Three weeks went by, and then I hurriedly started on the cape because time had run out faster than I'd realized. Out came the sewing machine, out came the patterned fabric, and I commenced. Two panels sewn together, then two more pinned to the first two, but wait. What was this? Two of the panels were now about four inches shorter than the other two, which was not possible, for I'd cut them all out together, hadn't adjusted the pattern any, and there was no one here to tamper with it but me. This couldn't be. I sat looking at that half-sewn cape for a long time, trying to figure it all out, but there was no logical explanation. It just was. That was my first solid clue that I had unseen company.

After my irritation subsided over wasted time and what would soon be wasted fabric—for now I'd now have to cut down the other two panel pieces—I did so and then sewed it all together. It turned out good . . . considering. A week later, the party commenced.

Samhain is a Celtic festival in remembrance of our ancestors, a time when the spirits of the dead and the Faeries travel back and forth from the Otherworld into ours because the veil between the worlds is thin. Halloween originated from this Celtic celebration, so to honor the ancestors was one of the reasons I was having the party; the other was to enjoy the company of my friends and family.

The party turned out to be a happy success, and when it was over, I had two friends offer to stay and help me clean the kitchen. They washed up and left everything on the counters so I could put it all away the next day, but a curious thing happened. A curved-handled spoon that had belonged to my mother disappeared in the process. I searched all the cupboards for that spoon, called most of my friends to ask if they had seen it or put it somewhere, but no one had, so where had it gone? Another mystery?

A few months later, I was reaching into the back of the bottom kitchen cupboard for a seldom-used casserole dish when I spied the vanished spoon in the far corner and wondered how this spoon grew legs and walked into the corner of a dark kitchen cupboard. I had no answers, but I had my suspicions, and I was happy to have my spoon back if for nothing else but sentimental value.

I started to notice other things mysteriously vanished and reappeared in strange places later: my gold ring that I always wore ended up at the bottom of a sweater drawer, my personal embroidered altar cloth was found behind a table in my studio, and when my wallet went missing, it showed up the next day lying inside the threshold of my bedroom door. Plus, other things that would matter to no one but me vanished and showed up later. In spite of all these disappearances, I didn't think much about it. I just figured I had an invisible houseguest of the Faery sort and occasionally left a bowl of milk and honey out overnight on the counter for him.

In my hallway there's a small four-shelved closet where I keep towels and bathroom things, and most of the time these things get moved in and out on a regular basis. The only light is a dim overhead bulb in the hall that's pretty useless, so I don't normally bother with it. This day I'd gone to the closet to put away some folded towels without turning on the light as it was light enough, and I knew where the towels went automatically. I opened the door, and *something* crawled—or rolled—off the towel shelf, hit the edge of my toe, and stopped right there at my feet, which made me jump back because I couldn't see what it was. My first thought was *Bug!* Not that I'm afraid of bugs, but it was dark and I was startled!

I stepped back and reached around the wall to turn on the light, and there on the floor was a small shiny marble. It didn't take me long to work out that a House Brownie was apparently living in my closet and greeting me, so I picked up the marble, said, "Hello" and "Thank you for the gift." Then I took it into the kitchen to examine it closer. It was a pretty thing, in what's called carnival glass, which is glass that's been sprayed with a metallic salt solution and fired to give it an exterior luster. When looking at it in normal light, it's blue, gold, and purple, but when you hold it up to a window or bright light, it's a beautiful solid shade of green—green like the forest, green like the Fae. Yes, I'd been given a gift in recognition of a relationship that I needed to appreciate more because few are privileged enough to have a Faery living in their closet, and to know about it.

Since then, the Brownie and I have become more aware of the space we share in the house, and I've learned to rely on him to recover lost items, like my glasses, car keys or the CD remote, which I seem to set down a lot and then don't remember where

I put them. I just ask him and SNAP! There they are! All he asks of me is an occasional bowl of milk and honey, or a cookie now and then—and to pretty much leave him alone in his closet—and all is well.

Once in a while, he'll turn on the touch-sensitive light of my china hutch because he likes to look at all the shiny glass and silver items glittering beneath it. I'm glad we finally got to know each other though because now I don't have to question if I'm losing my sanity or not—even though some people would have to concede that it's already a done deal. Oh well, they don't know the truth like I do!

CHAPTER 12
Woodland Elves

No one really knows the full history of the Elves except the Elves themselves, but even parts of that are vague and hazy in their memories, for they are a long-lived race and were created before time as we know it—though where and when is not clear. They are of a non-earthly creation and non-human blood, so how and why they ended up on our planet is an unanswered question that has been bandied about for centuries.

Physically they look similar to humans though more refined, but their inborn character is not like a human's nor are their lives guided by the same human principles or understandings.

Most Elves are tall with pale complexions, blond hair, and blue or gray eyes. Those with dark hair and brown eyes usually have ancestors from other cultures or are hybrids. Not all of them are beautiful though, for many are odd and strange-looking.

The Elven are not overly fond of humans and will make a concerted effort to keep away from them or totally disregard them altogether when they're around. There are exceptions to this thought, such as when a human has shown himself/herself to be in tune with the Elementals and has established a working relationship with nature and the nature spirits or has Elven blood.

There are certain factions of Elves that hold a great animosity towards humans and can be dangerous if you cross them. These groups are best avoided because they greatly enjoy messing with you if given half the chance. It's easy to make assumptions about who is or is not friendly, so just remember to be courteous and respectful to whomever you come across, which is the best course of action to adopt.

No Elves, of whichever faction, will deliberately go out of their way to do you harm because they have better things to do, but please do remember to keep this advice in mind.

Elves are extremely independent and self-governing and follow strictly adhered to rules that in no way reflect human rules nor do their lives reflect human lives. Their societies are egalitarian though they do have their nobility who help guide and keep the peace. They all have different specialties that are innate and individualized, such as weaving, storytelling, woodworking, beading, etc., and these specialties are utilized within their own kinship groups. Though they have what humans would call "money" in the form of gold, silver, and gems, mostly they use these for adornment rather than for exchange. The barter system is their main means of trade.

When among humans Elves will dress in similar fashion, but with their own kind, their clothing is always elegant but restrained, gearing towards more earthy colors, especially green. Sometimes their nobles wear white or red, but this is normally only when on important business while traveling.

In their relationships with others of their groups or clans, they do not marry like in the human world and they generally do not stay in monogamous relationship for extended lengths of time. Sex to them is a normal natural expression of their innate connection to all that is, the creative source. It is through this sexual energy/life-force energy/creative energy that they fuel their natural magical abilities to create. They transmute that sexual energy to spiritual energy then use it for more than just physical release, and this exists naturally for them. Their sexual instinct is unlike a human's primal sexual instinct because they are not driven by lust, bodily desires, or what humans call love. They seek only to create, whether it is another like themselves—which is not often an occurrence—or something beautiful and of worth to honor the Creator, for they are single-minded in being One with Source. The Elvish word for this is "Hulan," (pronounced Who-lawn). It is like the human "love," but not possessive, for it's a deeper connection than human love, which has lost its true meaning through misuse. The Elven don't "love" things or beings. They are Hulan—soul connected—with all things, for all things are of the Source.

Their nature is to be dignified, intelligent, curious, sensitive to pleasure, or suffering, unattached to physical reality, proud, studious, genuinely happy, playful, empathic, spontaneous, tireless when focused on a goal, sincere, and no-nonsense. They love variety and get bored easily when not engaged in a useful pursuit. Some say that they have a short attention span, but that is only because they are so long lived and unfading that the passage of time does not affect them, so nothing truly is new or untried, though it is always deeply felt. Beauty, music, and art in its many forms are paramount to them, as well as their connection to nature, which is where their source of truth lies.

On the flip side, they can be reserved, secretive, and suspicious when dealing with humans, but that only comes with their knowledge that they are misplaced here in the foreign world of humanity and are unable to return to their true home. That can make them appear sad and melancholic a lot of the time, and sometimes irritable even more.

They are slow to adjust to new or changed circumstances and don't care for anything that's not a part of their established tradition. Since they are such an old race and their culture has changed little over this long expanse of time, to others they seem archaic, but this lifestyle has been entirely by their choice. They have no need for those continually modern upgrades of what they perceive to be useless items or conveniences because they are perfectly content with what they know to be the tried and true.

Elves are very self-confident and totally themselves 100% of the time, and they feel no need to try to impress or get you to like them. If you do or don't matters not, for they'll always take it in stride. In the end they believe it's your problem one way or the other, and to humans this comes across as being cold and egotistical. In truth, it is just knowing who and what they are—which would be a good lesson for humans to learn also.

The Elves lead a magical life, and their magic is the thread that ties them to each other, their existence here on the earth and the Source from whence they came. Magic is a constant reality in their lives, woven into their very being, for it's not something they do but something they are. While humans "learn" magic and how to wield it, Elves just do it innately and don't think or consider it to be special or out of the ordinary. It's just a matter of need and then willing it so. Energy and the different vibrations of energy are manipulated in a way that serves them, but of course, always first being at One with the Source and the good that is connected to it.

Another aspect of Elven magic is Glamour. Glamour is a kind of illusionary magic that is used to disguise their own appearance as well as certain objects, such as their homes and communities. It's like a kind of enchantment in which a mild trance comes over humans and makes them tend to briefly "zone out" or react differently than they would to normal things or circumstances. The Elves don't do this to deceive but to keep control of a situation when humans are involved because humans have a difficult time being in their presence, tending to get silly and obtrusive.

Sometimes they use this Glamour as a protection and sometimes it's just to make things prettier and more appealing. Glamour is a natural allure the Elves have that is attractive to anyone who comes into contact with them. It is an elusive and mysterious power that entices, fascinates, and draws individuals into their aura. Humans with elven blood are less susceptible to glamour than full-blooded humans but not totally because the Elves don't often make a distinction between the two unless they know you personally.

The best way to keep from being *Glamoured* is to be aware of your surroundings and not take anything for granted. If you do find that you are feeling oddly out of sorts, spacey, or are agreeing to things you normally wouldn't, then you probably have been *Glamoured*. Don't worry though because Glamour doesn't have lasting effects. It normally wears off after the Elves have left.

Healing by the act of will and touch is a gift the Elven have always possessed. This they accomplish through channeling the energy of Source through their bodies and into the patient, healing the aura of the patient first and then concentrating on the physical body. It's a matter of enlivening the damaged tissue by summoning and then directing Source energy from the world of spirit and drawing the original energy pattern back into the wounded parts. Everything is just an echo of Source resonating at different levels of vibration, a living thing that holds all of creation together. Because Elves know how to maintain the balance of that vibration and be grateful for it, they are able to call back the life-force and the memory of its original form, thus weaving the broken or torn threads back together and making it whole again. They are also known to have balms that heal and bring others back to life if they have not completely passed the portal into death yet.

The Elves have their own language but will speak in the tongue of the beings around them. In truth, it is hard to tell an elf from a human if they choose to remain anonymous because they can blend in anywhere by adopting the ways and mannerisms of each place they visit. Humans with Fae-blood are more likely to recognize an elf in disguise, but not always—for they are so good at concealment that sometimes even they are confounded.

Because they are so closely related, Elves can talk with nature also. They have formed a bond between themselves and the nature spirits and work together to keep everything on the planet flowing smoothly. Most humans think that Elves and nature spirits always have a scent like flowers, and the nature spirits do, but the elven have a scent that is neither sweet, pungent, or any other recognizable scent. Rather it is a non-scent, for there are no other words to describe it, but it's definitely identifiable once first encountered. If they desire that you know they're around, they will send this scent out into the air as a greeting. If you smell it, be courteous and say hello. Yes, even if it's only into what you perceive as empty space because they have the power to blend into their surrounds and become invisible.

Remember to appreciate the creative works of art, like music, sculpture, literature, and painting that the Elves have blessed us with, for many of these masterpieces have been created by the magic of the elven folk themselves. If they had not kindly done so, our world would be a sadder, more barren place indeed.

If you think that Glamour is something the Elves only do to the unaware, think again. They also can slip one over on those of us who know what to look for. Don't kid yourself. Everyone is susceptible to their charm, and here's my own mildly embarrassing example.

Elven Glamour

It was raining and had been since early morning, softly blowing sideways with the wind and crying through tree branches as it built up shallow in the street gutters.

A warm autumn sun finally peeked out from behind the clouds around 11:30, testifying to a warmer drier afternoon. I picked up my walking stick from the gathering basket and headed out to the woods hoping to find the peace and quiet I usually found there.

Crossing the road then down the street, I stopped and stood facing the sun as its embrace gently kissed my face. I was happy.

Once inside the forest, I found a deer path and followed it, weaving through the trees and slowly making my way towards a favored spot, happily oblivious to what awaited me. Turning left, I thought I heard voices and then the piercing sounds of a wood grinder and chain saw screaming on the wind—or maybe it wasn't the saw screaming. Maybe it was something "Other." As I stepped back onto the road, I saw the source of the wailing noise—for people and machines were making scars on the face of the forest floor. A volunteer group was tearing away the "invasive" plants and trees—this time the hackberry and weeping elm were the targets. I could feel them crying from within, big tears falling from each limb and leaf. I stopped and tried to talk with one of the park workers to get them to make sense of it for me, but she was having none of it.

"Can't there be just one place left wild?" I asked her. "Just one?"

"You must be Victoria," she questioned with a forced smile. Apparently she'd heard of me. I was going to get nowhere; I could tell.

This wasn't the first person I had ever talked with among the park commission members to try to get a better management plan going for the removal of what they considered "invasives." Usually I was received with one form or another of temporary pacification just to get me out of their hair. Nothing ever changed within their own fixed ideas of how the forest was to be managed.

Today was not the day for me to try again because I just wasn't up to it after this encounter. I'd started off with a song in my heart and a yearning for connection, but presently I felt like a deflated balloon with no air left to continue on through the sky. I needed solitude so I could call my energies back and grieve for the loss of life, so I turned and walked off. No birds flew here now or sang through the trees, only the shriek of a chain saw whining in my ears.

With aching heart I wearily made my way towards the Zelkovas and sat on the bench below them. These trees had always brought to my mind Tolkien's mallorn trees. No, they weren't as magnificent as he described the mallorns to be, but their gray scaly bark and lacey overhead leaf pattern made me feel that a magical presence was there dwelling beyond normal human perception, a Fae presence that was interwoven within the consciousness of the place. I always found comfort here. While I sat there, tears rose in my eyes, and I let out a sigh to lend voice to my pain.

Then out loud to the spirits of the place I prayed, "I've tried all these years to get someone to listen. I've done all I can do. I can do no more, for I am weary of struggling against this wanton destruction of nature. I'm sorry; I have no more in me to fight with. Truly, I am overwhelmed with sadness, but I am spent!" It was the last cry of a dying soul, for I could carry no more weight of it.

Sitting among the calming energy of the zelkovas, I turned and saw strangers about 150 feet behind me on the path making their way in my direction.

Great, I thought, for I wasn't in the mood to smile and act pleasant, and I certainly wasn't in the mood at the moment for conversation. I just wanted to be alone, so I sat quietly waiting for them to pass.

It shouldn't have taken them long to reach me, but time suddenly seemed to stand still because five minutes later, I glanced back and found they had only moved about ten feet. It was as if space had unfolded and kept them distanced from me, making me feel odd and unable to grasp what was truly happening.

Then abruptly, like space had now folded inward again, they were almost in front of me. I was drawn into a kind of energy field in which their Glamour had thrown a mantle over my reality and hypnotized me. (In retrospect, I hadn't realized it at the time.)

There were four of them, young males—early twenties I guessed, tall, and good-looking. From a distance, I could see there was nothing particularly unusual about the way they looked or what they wore, for they all had on denim jeans like most young guys wore. The only thing that seemed out of place to me was their long thigh length jackets, which were dark green in color, except one and his was white. If you know anything about the Elves, green has always been their color, and this is one reason some people won't wear it. Sometimes, though, Elves do wear white, but that's usually only if they are from a noble family line.

The one in white started to walk by . . . *walk*—that hardly seems the appropriate term now because they never really appeared to walk anywhere. They were just there . . . and then gone.

He unexpectedly turned towards me, smiled, and said, "Hello."

I don't normally speak to strangers when I'm in the woods, but he felt familiar, like we'd met before, and I was not myself at that moment though didn't know it at the time.

I smiled back and said, "Hi."

"Taking a walk in the forest?" I asked. It came out before I had a chance to consider. *Wasn't I, just a second before, trying to avoid verbal exchange with anyone?* I wondered to myself.

All four of them were now together on the path directly in front of me, leaning up against the railing of the observation bench where I sat. Something came over me, and I wanted to engage them in conversation. I wanted them to stay there and talk with me, for they had a dignity about them, an Otherworld Faeness that enticed me and drew me in.

"Enjoying it here in spite of that?" and I pointed in the direction of where the plant removal was occurring.

I could see them clearer now. Three of them had long hair past their shoulders, two dark brown, one blond. The fourth was taller than the rest, and his head was totally shaved. He appeared to be the leader, though I don't know why I felt that way about him. I just did. The one in white affirmed that yes, what was happening was sad, for the act was totally unnccessary.

How did he know what I was talking about? Had they also stood witnessing, feeling the sadness that oozed out of the air itself? Did they hear the cruel voice of the chain saw on the wind? I wondered.

I was shocked that they understood what I meant and more shocked that they would agree, for they didn't appear to think or act like what my preconceived notion of twenty-somethings thought or acted like. They were polite, respectful, attentive, soft-spoken and genuinely concerned about the forest and the destruction going on inside it.

For a brief moment, I thought he was mocking me. "Are you being sarcastic?" I asked.

What was I doing? I quickly questioned myself, for these four were perfect strangers, and maybe I should be more guarded— and courteous—but in the end I really felt no fear or embarrassment being around them or saying exactly what came to my mind.

"No, absolutely not," he said back. "It's awful what goes on in the wild places and that humans feel the need to micro-manage nature."

I almost fell off the bench in wonder. Mostly, I found that there weren't many from outside my own intimate circle of friends that ever thought nature didn't need to be controlled in some way to keep it from getting unruly like a bunch of misbehaved children. Granted, you didn't want nature growing wild all over the place because we all had to live in a somewhat maintained environment, but there was a healthy balance that could be obtained. It was just considering all the options and then finding that balance.

"Oh, thank the gods!" I said sincerely. "Someone besides me thinks what they're doing is wrong!"

All four of them chimed in that, yes, they felt the same way. That opened up the door for me to expound upon the whole affair and how I saw the unnecessary abuse of the land as a relevant environmental issue in our present society.

After so much of this kind of talk, most people usually get tired of the subject and want to change topics or leave. I was anticipating this, so I said, "Well, I could go on and on, but I'm sure you don't want to hear it."

"I do," replied one of the dark-haired ones, and he walked briskly up and sat down next to me on the bench as the other three followed.

If I were in my normal frame of mind, I would have been uncomfortable about the direction this had turned because I was now trapped there on the observation bench with no getting out, but I felt perfectly safe and at ease, no worries. The whole situation was surrealistic, for these four seemed very Otherworldly, and I must have been under some kind of enchantment because I gave nothing that was happening a second thought; I had just jumped right in, which is something I never did.

Twenty minutes passed as our conversation ran along the lines of nature, humans, the environment, and how life worked perfectly like the cogs of a wheel when everything was running smoothly and in balance. They all listened politely when I spoke and graciously commented when they had something to say, but the taller one—the one I felt was the leader—said more than the others did. When I questioned them about their backgrounds, he told me he was going to school to get his degree in environmental studies so that he could stop this sort of blind destruction and help the natural world. Upon asking the other three where they lived and if they were going to school, they masterfully avoided the question, like they didn't want to tell me the truth but didn't want to lie either.

Finally the guy in white said, "He's going," and he pointed to the guy sitting next to me. "He's trying to find himself," he continued with a smile.

I felt like there was some secret between them that they weren't willing to share at the moment, but rather than pursue it, I let it go.

As our conversation came back to the natural world and how we all felt that humans seemed to picture themselves as being more evolved than nature, which gave them the right to rule over it and decide what stays and what goes, I quoted one of my favorite quotes about hollyhocks and how viewing them one way makes them weeds and viewing them another way makes them flowers. But before I finished the last sentence, the "leader" had finished it for me.

How did he know the end line? Had he read the book? I pondered.

"Is that James ---?" (The last name I can't remember now) he asked me. "He's a poet from the 60's."

"No, that is a quote by Jim Thompson," I replied.

"Oh," he smiled and said rather sheepishly.

Again I wondered how he knew to finish the quote if he didn't appear to know where it came from? And why would he think of someone from the sixties, for I was a product of that era and was it so obvious that he'd chosen a poet from that time frame? If so, why? This was getting more mysterious, for it was the third thing he apparently knew without seeming to have any prior knowledge. The second one happened as he finished my own sentence for me when I was talking about the invasive plants being removed.

I had said, "The park workers clear off the areas of underbrush that they consider invasive, and after they do, people walk into these areas when they shouldn't and never have before, which compacts the soil, scares the animals, destroys the new growth by stepping on it, and they . . ."

"Throw their trash around," he finished.

Ok, can he read minds, or does he see me picking up trash when he is in the inner-dimension? Even though I was still in a somewhat enchanted fog, I was coherent enough to have this come to mind and question it.

"Yes, I have a problem with the invasive plant removal," I stated rather vehemently.

"The only thing invasive on this planet is humans," he said looking at me knowingly.

That was it. I was jarred senseless, for that is the exact thing I was going to say next. It was my favorite line when talking about such matters, which added up to mystery #4 because he knew exactly what I was going to say next.

The fog over me was beginning to lift because I was seriously starting to question what was going on. They must have sensed this because they suddenly got up to leave.

"Well, we have to go. It was nice talking with you. Perhaps we'll see you again, here or in a future place."

The leader smiled at me like he already knew my future. Then he said, "Good-bye, friend."

They all got up and started walking towards the grove of redwood trees where my Beltaine encounter happened. It's a spot situated on a curve of the path that leads around to the cork and oak trees. But I wasn't ready to see them leave yet. I was drawn to keep that connection going because I felt energetically pinned inside their energy, and it was so refreshing and pure—like how a spring rain cleans the air, and everything is fresh and new.

"What are your names?" I questioned as they walked off, for I was trying to say anything to tempt them into continuing the conversation, but they never answered, just kept walking, and then waved one last time as they rounded the curve.

I sat there for just a minute, trying to collect myself, for I knew something wonderful had just happened, but I couldn't quite grasp the implications.

Then I thought, *Wait, if they are who I think they are, I have some things I want to ask them.* So I jumped up and headed around the curve also, but they were nowhere to be seen. Not more than two minutes had passed, and there was no way they could have moved along that fast, except they were gone, vanished, almost as if the earth had swallowed them up!

I was clear headed now. The fog had finally risen off my mind, and I was upset at myself for seemingly to have sleepwalked through the whole affair. There were so many wonderful things I could have found out, so many mysteries standing right in front of me that could have been revealed.

What had come over me? I knew better than to walk around in the forest daydreaming because you can miss some great life-changing opportunities if you do. *Had I been bewitchment by them, or had I put myself to sleep?* Looking back, I had to concede that it must have been them, for I'd been taught by my teachers and guides not to be duped by the Elves and go to sleep. If you're awake and alert enough to see it, wonder is often right around the corner—though in certain situations, everyone knows hindsight is often 20/20. Let me tell you though, even if I was helplessly under their Glamour, I think I might have missed out on some really great information!

CONCLUSION

And so at this point in my life, I had come full circle. From my birth—and in that birth a sleeping and forgetting—I had slowly awakened to find an understanding of my spiritual heritage—my roots—and returned home to walk again under the shadow of Mt. Shasta and stand at the beginning of the old forgotten pathway that gradually wound down over a hump of gray stone and into the meadow green.

The Shasta Vortex was my beginnings, for I was conceived and birthed among the mysteries of that manifest power of earth energy. It wasn't the beginning of our family's connection to the Faery realm, but it was a re-confirmation of an already planted seed. I was now among the energies that resonated with mine, and I felt a sense of relief, for so much time had passed and was lost. How I had missed home.

There are some that have walked the forgotten pathway into Faery and kept still while others have walked and later told their tales: James M. Barrie, P.L. Travers, Hans Christian Anderson, Lewis Carroll, J.R.R. Tolkien, and the Reverend Robert Kirk just to name a few, for they've all had a glimpse— or a stay—in the enchanted realms of the Faery folk.

Faery can be close or miles away, depending on your beliefs. It can lie in the laughter of children, the merry lilt of a joyful song, the toast to a new life come—or gone—and in the dance that weaves together the fates of all. It can lie in the crumbling hill forts of Scotland, the mountain peaks of Snowdonia, the frozen landscapes of Russia, and in your own back yard. When you do find Faery, it will always have been the last place you looked and the last step you took before giving up, for that's the way it works in the Blessed Lands.

Finding the Greenwood has never been easy, and proving yourself true is a must. Watchers guard the gates to keep the naysayers from entering—those who would throw stones at the heart of things. Don't bother to wear masks to conceal, for they know how to glimpse beyond and around and through. What the Otherworld asks for is a guardian and champion to stand up for the earth and nature—someone to hold strongly to the nearly forgotten realms of dreams, visions, and imaginations where those who know endeavor to walk the paths that run parallel into the country of Faery.

Don't let doubt cloud your judgment as so many have done; doubt is bred from fear, and fear causes us to never take chances. Trust and be willing to open to the possibilities of the lands of Faery, and you can open the door to a whole new way of living in the magic, one in which the Faeries have a place. How could that ever be something to regret or fear? If you ask any of those who've been there, they'll tell you that Faery is a place that resides in the land and always in the heart, for the child in us lives on through that blessed realm of enchantment, the land of the Otherworld.

So if you do find and open the door, stepping through as so many of us have done, just remember to be respectful as you would in any foreign country. Don't take anything with you when leaving, and if by chance you find yourself unable to get back, turn your clothes inside out, cut a doorway with an iron knife, and you'll be fine. Oh, and happy traveling!

Tell them I said, "Hello!"

APPENDIX ONE
Non-human and Human/Faery Hybrids:
Attributes and Characteristics

➢ They are naturally gifted in the arts, such as music, storytelling, painting, writing, sculpture, etc.

➢ They have a special "glow" or "shine" coming from within, like an inner light.

➢ They have a keen sense of humor, never seen to lose their childlike enthusiasm and sense of fun, and are full of good-natured mischief, but they can also be quiet and retiring.

➢ Humans are naturally drawn to them though they can't understand or explain why.

➢ They have a profound knowledge of all different areas of life and existence but have a hard time living within the confines of time schedules and what would be seen as the "normal" everyday routines of life.

➢ Spend a good deal of time in nature, either within their own yards and gardens or out in the wild places.

➢ They are distinctly male and female but don't always identify themselves with being of a certain sex, for they have a natural balance of male and female energy and are wholly themselves in that balance.

➢ They are generally neutral and objective.

➢ They are very curious, appear eccentric at times, and follow their own instincts and inner perceptions throughout their lives rather than adhere to what society dictates.

➢ Humans often find them odd, puzzling, mysterious, and aloof.

➢ They perceive things beyond the five senses, which are usually heightened, and can sense things far before anyone else can.

➢   They have a profound need for quietness and solitude. Humans often perceive them as being lonely, which they aren't because they are constantly connected with the Otherworld though at times they appear to carry a deep unexplainable sadness.

➢   They look younger and age more slowly than most other humans.

➢   They often feel as though they are out of place in the mundane world that most others live comfortably in. They have a sense of being dislocated or in the wrong time and place.

➢   They have a strong distrust of humans and never reveal themselves unless a long and abiding friendship has been established—and sometimes they never do.

➢   Most have an ethereal beauty and charm that cannot be defined, which can also depend on the caste they come from. Their eyes are striking and unusual in some way, either in shape, color, or depth of soul.

➢   They tend to shy away from technology and don't relate much to things that take them away from their natural connections with the world of nature, desiring instead to live more in the old ways, but if no other choice is given, they adapt very well to what is required.

➢   Most don't care to be in large crowds of people and avoid human physical contact as much as possible, unless it is with a mate, which they do not require but make as a conscious choice to learning.

➢   They are restless and have a longing for something they can't quite place.

➢   They have a hard time dealing with human emotions and knowing how to handle them because in the land of Faery, emotions do not exist in the same way. They come into the human world to learn, and humans can, in turn, learn from them if allowed.

➢ They have a natural code of honor that is beyond most human understanding or ability to adhere to.

➢ They are often accused of being without natural affection or morals, but that is only because human laws and Faery laws differ considerably, and the Faery, though in a human body, doesn't see anything wrong, for they live by the instincts which are inherent to them.

➢ The cartilage extension of their upper ear edge can have a slight crease or angle to it. Science has named this ear peak after Charles Darwin and called it Darwin's Peak. They say it's an evolutionary leftover of the pointed mammal ear, but it's more frequently a sign of a non-human embodiment—that and slightly rounded sloping fingernails.

➢ They can have acute allergies and intolerances to foods and certain metal alloys, such as brass, steel, or iron. For some, piercings of any sort are out of the question because their bodies can react badly to them.

Kiss The Wind

APPENDIX TWO
The Dos and Don'ts of the Faery Realms

✓   Don't go blundering through the Faery lands like you own them. One of the things they don't appreciate in humans is their arrogance.

✓   If you come across a Faery being who is busy or appears to be conversing with another, don't interrupt. If you truly feel the need to speak with the Faery, wait patiently until you are noticed, and then speak only if you're invited.

✓   Don't be loud, aggressive, demanding, or pushy. The Fae expect kindness, patience, and respect just like anyone does.

✓   Don't take anything with you when you leave the Faery lands unless it is given to you by the Fae.

✓   If a spirit or Faery being ignores you, don't try to strike up a conversation and get to know them. Move on.

✓   Remember that the Faery beings can be helpful, but they can also be sly and tricky. Don't expect them to act like humans, for their laws and their ways are not like ours. Plus, they enjoy playing games that confuse and bewilder.

✓   It's been debated for years whether it's safe to eat anything offered you while in the Faery realms. Some say yes, some no. For safety's sake, if you're offered food, graciously decline.

✓   Be a happy and optimistic person, for the Faeries will be more willing to work with you if you have a positive attitude. Negativity only decreases your energy vibration, which won't match where you are or what you're trying to accomplish. If you keep that up, you'll find yourself unable to pass the portal into the lands of the Fae.

✓   If you find yourself being pursued against your will by a Faery being, cross a body of water like a pond or stream.

✓ If you set up a meeting with a Faery, make sure to stick to it because they do not understand the idea of "forgetting" or "having something else to do" and consider those excuses rude.

✓ If you accidentally wander into the Faery realms, turn your clothes inside out, cut a doorway with an iron knife, and never get angry about losing your way. Eventually the Faeries will tire of confusing you and open the gateway back into the physical world.

✓ At times the Faeries will be happy to see you, and at other times they won't. When you feel unwelcome, come back another day and try again.

✓ Don't expect to work with the Faeries under the influence of drugs or alcohol. The Fae have a low tolerance for humans who cannot control their own weaknesses and will shut the portal into the Otherworld so fast it will make your head spin. Truly, you do not want to make them angry, and this sort of nonsense will.

✓ Do take a gift or offering of friendship when you go to Faery, for this shows respect and a willingness to give graciously, not just receive.

✓ Do read the myths and legends of the Celtic people and the Faery folk before you travel into the Faery lands. Knowing the habits and customs of any foreign land is wise if you want to be welcomed. Be prepared to tell a story or two while there because the Fae love to hear about their own personal adventures and history.

✓ Do respect and honor the natural world, for it is the dwelling place of the Faeries, and they are directly connected with it, so respecting their home, as well as your own, shows that you are sensitive to the needs of others besides yourself.

✓ Be open and willing to learn from the Faeries, for they have much to teach humans.

APPENDIX THREE
Wordology of Faery

ALCHEMY:

Word derived from the ancient Egyptian name "Khem," meaning black after the blackness of the Egyptian soil. Also known as the Divine Art or Hermetic Art based on the spiritual and philosophical concept that precise correspondence occurs between the visible and invisible worlds/the worlds of matter and spirit that can be accessed through certain techniques to transform the base metal of ignorance into the gold of wisdom. Symbolized physically by turning lead into gold. In alchemy, the physical world is a reflection of the spiritual world. "As above, so below."

ALTERED STATE OF CONSCIOUSNESS:

Shift in the normal waking state of consciousness when the speed of brain wave activity slows down, and the unconscious mind takes over, like during meditation, hypnosis, dream state, or trance. There are four brain state frequencies: beta, alpha, theta and delta. Beta level: complete waking consciousness. Alpha level: information from the subconscious is available to the mind, such as during daydreaming, light trance, or meditation (the level of brainwave frequency in which to journey to the Otherworld). Theta level: drowsiness and light sleep, vague awareness of what is happening around you. Delta level: deep dreamless sleep state

BAY/LAUREL:

Two interchangeable names for the same plant, known for its exalted status because of its association with the Greek sun god Apollo. A tree of protection said to dispel evil spirits, guard against thunder and lightning strikes, and is the primary herb used to ensure safe travel and increased psychic awareness of the other dimensions of reality not available through the normal five senses.

BELTAINE:

A Celtic festival that cycles into the summer months and is celebrated on May 1st. The season for celebrating sexuality, fertility, and spring. A time when the veil between the world of humans and Faeries is thin. Also, known as May Day.

BETWIXT AND BETWEEN:

The place between our perceived reality and the Otherworld, generally found at "in between" places, such as a fork in the road, the edge of a stream or sea, noon and midnight, dawn and dusk, holy wells, Samhain, Beltaine, bridges, or any place that is neither here in our physical world nor there in the other.

CAST CIRCLE/SACRED SPACE:

Creating a sacred space or casting a circle—done to energetically create a place in which to work a rite or ritual. Similar to using focused energy to visualize the creation of a special imaginary room in which to do spiritual work. Circle—symbolic of the ever circling round of eternity or that which is without end.

CELTIC:

Six modern day European cultures that are identified and connected with the Celtic languages: Ireland/Irish-Gaelic, Scotland/Scottish-Gaelic, Wales/Welsh, Cornwall/Cornish, The Isle of Man/Manx, and Brittany/Breton.

CHAKRA:

Sanskrit word meaning "wheel." Invisible energy in the body that weaves together and forms seven major vortices/energy centers that spin and are the focal points for specific types of energy:

1.   Base or Root Chakra. Located at the base of the spine and associated with the basic life instincts. Also where kundalini energy is stored. Color—red.

2.　　Sacral Chakra. Located just below the navel and related to close relationships, sexuality, and lower emotions. Color— orange.

3.　　Solar Plexus Chakra. Located above the navel and below the breastbone. Governs the emotions, helps control and direct energy, and is the seat of our power. Color—yellow.

4.　　Heart Chakra. Located at the center of the chest and governs higher emotions, such as love, selflessness, authenticity, and compassion. Gateway between the upper and lower three chakras and where we find our balance between the physical and the spiritual. Color—green.

5.　　Throat Chakra. Located at the center of the throat and helps us communicate, and speak our truths. Related to things like creativity and expression. Color—electric blue.

6.　　Third-eye Chakra. Located between our eyebrows and governs mediumship abilities and psychic communication, intelligence, higher creativity, non-physical sight—the ability to see spirit, Faeries, and other non-humans. Also called the Second Sight. Color—indigo.

7.　　Crown Chakra. Located at the top of the head and connects us to the Higher Powers. Governs spiritual consciousness, Divine realization, and complete fulfillment and understanding. Color—either purple or white.

CLAIRVOYANCE:

Derived from the French word that means "clear seeing" and refers to the ability to see into the past, present, or future with inner/psychic vision.

COLLECTIVE UNCONSCIOUS:

That part of the unconscious mind common to all humans— shares memories, mental patterns and images consisting of a perfect model for instinctual behavior known as archetypes, which form the basic outline for the human personality. Totality of human consciousness, available symbolically in dreams, archetypes, visions, meditations, intuition, etc., to guide humankind toward self-fulfillment.

CORACLE:

A small, round, wood or wicker boat covered in leather that is stretched over the frame and propelled by a paddle.

DREAMTIME:

Specifically an Australian Aboriginal belief in a psychic realm that is shared by everyone and resembling the collective unconscious concept. Shared by most indigenous societies. Similar to the Celtic belief of the Otherworld where the gods, Faeries, and Spirits of the Dead dwell and the Native American Dreamtime that is also a parallel universe/reality holding all levels of awareness that can be accessed through an altered state of conscious, i.e., meditation, dreams, trance, and journeying. Also, a state of consciousness reached when sleeping.

ELEMENTAL:

Spirits composed of only one element: air, earth, fire, or water. Also, sometimes used to describe nature spirits, such as Elves, Dwarfs, Leprechauns, etc.

ELF:

Derived from the Norse "Âlfr," Anglo-Saxon "Alf," and High German "Alp." Thought by different folk traditions either to be from the realm of the Faeries or a caste unto themselves but known to be ancient beings who wander freely across the lands at one with the world of nature where they remain hidden from prying eyes when they choose. Appear as they wish and can enter human evolution and interact with them in ways that can be strange, beguiling, but also mysterious.

FAIRY/FAERY:

English word derived from the French "fée." Powerful beings of the world of nature who were regarded as divine and should be treated with respect and some caution. Beings that help sustain nature and participate in keeping it thriving on this planet. Also known in Celtic cultures as the Sidhe, the Gentry, the Hidden People, People of Peace, Fair Folk, Shining Ones, Luminescent Ones, the Good People, People of the Hills, Wee Folk, Daoine Sith, Tylwyth Teg, etc.

Can also be a place/realm, as well as a being. Often perceived as being within the earth, in another dimension, or a parallel reality.

FÉE/FAE: (Pronounced Fay)

A French word derived from the Latin word fatare, meaning fate, or to enchant. Another word for a Faery being.

Also, an out-of-the-ordinary feeling, usually associated with a particular area where the world of humans and Faeries intersect.

GLAMOUR:

Illusionary charms to attract, conceal, and disguise. The gift, power, and ability to tempt, fascinate, and draw something or someone to you.

INVOCATION:

Prayer or petition to a higher power to open oneself to a heightened state of consciousness for a specific purpose. A formal plea or request.

INVOKE:

To call forth, invite, or ask an entity for assistance through invocation/prayer.

JOURNEYING:

Going into an altered state of consciousness and traveling out-of-body into a parallel universe/reality/time/space to gain wisdom, knowledge, and healing for others or self.

LEY LINES:

Lines of energy that run across and beneath the earth and connect various sites, such as earthen mounds, standing stones, circular moats, castles, wells, churches, trees and crossroads. Said to carry healing energy and be of spiritual and astrological significance.

ONE FOOT ON EACH SIDE OF THE RIVER:

Living in the mundane world as well as in the Otherworld, which is also known as living between the worlds, where a being is physically in this one but spiritually and intuitively in the Other.

OTHERWORLD:

The land of the Faeries, gods, ancestors, and the dead. Spiritual dimensions that are part of the manifest world we live in, closely woven with it and not removed from it. A place where the deities and non-humans dwell.

QUINTESSENSE:

An addition to the four Elements of life: Earth, Air, Fire, and Water mentioned by the ancient occult philosophers, alchemists, and magicians. The fifth element called the Quintessence, "Aether," Spirit, Life Principle, or Life-Force Energy. Called "Azoth" by the early Egyptians to mean the measureless spirit of life that came from the other regions of the universe or the Divine Source from which all creation stems.

RITUAL/RITE:

Ceremonial procedure performed to achieve the specific goals of its practitioner.

SAMHAIN: (Pronounced Sow-un)

Means "summer's end." Known popularly as Halloween. The last of three Celtic harvest festivals celebrated on October 31st. Celebrates the end of the harvest season, the change from summer to winter, and the beginning of a new year. Another potent time when the veil between the world of humans and Faeries is thin.

SIDHE: (Pronounced Shee)

A cairn, hill, or mound, place where Faeries dwell, also called Faery mounds, now synonymous with their name. Home of the Irish Tuatha De Danann, the old gods turned Faery that are now call the Sidhe.

SURFACE WORLD:

The manifest land where humans dwell.

TALISMAN:

From the Greek *telesma* meaning to consecrate or complete. Any consecrated object that brings luck and averts negativity, like a good luck charm worn or something kept for its magical power.

THE OAKEN DOOR/DOOR WITH NO KEY:

The Celtic spiritual portal into another dimension where Otherworld beings dwell.

TIR NA N'OG:

"Land of the Young." Irish name for the Otherworld.

VORTEX:

A whirling mass of energy that causes a vacuum at its center, into which anything caught in its motion is drawn. These vortexes are high energy concentrations that originate from a magnetic or spiritual source and are part of the power of earth. Also, considered to be gateways to the spiritual and dimensional realms. Exist where there are concentrations of irregular gravity manifestations and are associated with ley lines, energy lines that cross the earth.

Well-known sites of vortex activity: Stonehenge in England; four sites in Sedona, Arizona; the Mt. Shasta, California vortex; the Oregon Vortex in Gold Hill, Oregon; and the Superstition Mountains near Apache Junction, Arizona.

WHEEL OF THE YEAR/CYCLICAL WHEEL:

Recognized and honored by different earth-centered Traditions, Cycles and Seasons of the earth marked and celebrated in observance of the four solar holidays of the Winter and Summer Solstice and the Spring and Fall Equinoxes and the four Celtic cross-quarter festivals of Imbolc, Beltaine, Lughnassadh and Samhain.

FURTHER READING

Arrowsmith, Nancy. *Field Guide to the Little People: A Curious Journey into the Hidden Realm of Elves, Faeries, Hobgoblins and Other Not-So-Mythical Creatures.* Woodbury, Minnesota: Llewellyn Publications, 2009.

Campanelli, Pauline. *Ancient Ways: Reclaiming Pagan Traditions.* St. Paul, Minnesota: Llewellyn Worldwide, Ltd., 1991.

Cunningham, Scott. *Wicca: A Guide for the Solitary Practitioner.* St. Paul, Minnesota: Llewellyn Publications, 1998.

Emerson, Willis George. *The Smoky God.* Mundelein, Illinois: Palmer Publications, Inc., 1965.

Evans-Wentz, W. Y. *The Fairy-Faith in Celtic Countries.* Mineola, New York: Dover Publications, Inc., 2002.

Ferguson, Diana. *The Magickal Year: A Pagan Perspective on the Natural World.* UK: Labyrinth Publishing (UK) Ltd., 1996.

Goodman, Linda. *Linda Goodman's Sun Signs.* New York, New York: Bantam Books, 1971.

Gregory, Lady. *Gods & Fighting Men.* Toronto, Ontario: Macmillan Company of Canada Limited, 1976.

Guest, Charlotte E. *The Mabinogion.* New York: Barnes and Noble Publishing, Inc., 2005.

Hawkens, Paul. *The Magic of Findhorn.* London: Souvenir Press LTD., 1975.

Hunt, Victoria. *Animal Omens.* Woodbury, MN: Llewellyn Worldwide, Ltd., 2008.

Kelly, Penny. *The Elves of Lily Hill Farm: A Partnership with Nature.* Lawton, MI: Lily Hill Publishing, 1997.

Knight, Sirona. *Celtic Traditions: Druids, Faeries, and Wiccan Rituals.* New York, NY: Kensington Publishing Corp., 2000.

MacManus, Dermot. *The Middle Kingdom.* Gerrards Cross, Buckinghamshire: Colin Smythe Limited, 1973.

Moorey, Teresa. *The Fairy Bible: The Definitive Guide to the World of Fairies.* New York, New York: Sterling Publications, 2008.

O'Hara, Gwydion. *Pagan Ways: Finding Your Spirituality in Nature.* St. Paul, MN: Llewellyn Publications, 1997.

Thomas, W. Jenkyn. *The Welsh Fairy Book,* Mineola, New York: Dover Publications, Inc., 2001.

White, Suzanne. *The New Astrology.* New York, NY: St, Martin's Press, 1986.

BIBLIOGRAPHY

Air-Alchemy Symbol. Retrieved from online. http://paganwiccan.about.com/od/bookofshadows/ig/Pagan-and-Wiccan-Symbols/Air.htm n.d. Web. 18 Oct. 2012.

Altars and Casting Circles. Retrieved from online. http://www.paganshire.com/Portals/0/Circle_with_alter.jpg n.d. Web. 21 Oct. 2012.

Ancient Solar Cross. Retrieved from online. http://paganwiccan.about.com/od/bookofshadows/ig/Pagan-and-Wiccan-Symbols/Solar-Cross.htm n.d. Web. 23 Sept. 2012.

Carmichael, Alexander. *Carmina Gadelica.* Vols. 1-6. Edinburg: Oliver and Boyd, 1940.

Clip Art ETC. Retrieved from online. http://etc.usf.edu/clipart/2200/2288/salamander1.html n.d. Web. 23 Aug. 2012.

Culpeper, Nicholas. *Culpeper's Complete Herbal.* Yeovil Road, Slough, Bucks, England: W. Foulsham & Co., LTD., n.d.

Cunningham, Scott. *Encyclopedia of Magical Herbs,* St. Paul, Minnesota: Llewellyn Publications, 2002.

Earth-Alchemy Symbol. Retrieved from online. http://paganwiccan.about.com/od/bookofshadows/ig/Pagan-and-Wiccan-Symbols/Earth.html n.d. Web. 18 Oct. 2012.

Elemental Undine. Retrieved from online. http://www.absolutearts.com/portfolios/e/emmett/ n.d. Web. 24 Sept. 2012.

Fire Symbol. Retrived from online. http://paganwiccan.about.com/od/bookofshadows/ig/Pagan-and-Wiccan-Symbols/Fire.html n.d. Web. 18 Oct. 2012.

Fortune, Dion. *Psychic Self-Defense.* York Beach, Main: Samuel Weiser, Inc., 1977.

Gnomes Images. Retrieved from online http://bellaterreno.com/graphics/clipart_mystical/gnome/default.html n.d.Web. 22 Aug. 2012

Kiersey, David & Bates, Marilyn. *Please Understand Me.* Del Mar, CA: Prometheus Nemesis Book Co., 1984.

Pagan Sabbaths Symbol. Retrieved from online. http://pendragon343.com/sabbats-ext.html n.d. Web. 20 Aprl 2013.

People of the Mounds. Retrieved from online. http://celticsociety.freeservers.com/sidhe.html/ n.d. Web. 24 Sept. 2012.

Slyphs. Retrieved from online. http://sylphsandufocloudships.wordpress.com/ n.d. Web. 17 Oct. 2012.

The Phoenix Bird Stencil. Retrieved from online. www.spraypaintstencils.com n.d. Web. 23 Aug. 2012.

Water Symbol. Retrieved from online. http://paganwiccan.about.com/od/bookofshadows/ig/Pagan-and-Wiccan-Symbols/Water.html n.d. Web. 18 Oct. 2012.

Yeats, W. B. *The Celtic Twilight, Myth, Fantasy and Folklore.* Bridport, Dorset: Prim Press, 1893.

ABOUT THE AUTHOR

I was fortunate enough to have been born at the foot of the fifth highest mountain peak in California, Mt. Shasta, which is one of several spiritual vortexes throughout the world.

A vortex is a whirling mass of energy that causes a vacuum at its center into which anything caught in its motion is drawn in. They are also considered to be gateways into and out of other spiritual and dimensional realms.

As an intuitive child who was blessed to be able to live a life in the country among fields, orchards, creeks, rivers – and in summer – lakes and the sea, I grew upon loving nature and knowing of the connection we shared. My Grandparents owned a small farm next to our home, and so I was also able to learn about animals and growing our own food.

I spend many hours wandering out-of-doors, honing my ability to talk with nature and the nature spirits. And they have taught me much!

When I got older, I started getting interested in the Norse Runes and using them for divinatory purposes, and I have been working seriously with them these past 17 years.

In 2003, I studied and received my Reiki Mastery, which I have incorporated into my own personal practice of healing with the power of nature.

2008 brought the publication of my first book Animal Omens, which was published by Llewellyn Worldwide Publishing.

Life has brought me many blessings, and I consider myself lucky to be able to share them with you. Please let me know if you have any questions or concerns.

Email: www.animalomens@yahoo.com

or find me on Facebook at:

www.facebook.com/v.hunt
www.facebook.com/thefaelandrealm

Aman-n, and Bright Blessings!

Other Books By Ozark Mountain Publishing, Inc.

Dolores Cannon
Conversations with Nostradamus,
  Volume I, II, III
Jesus and the Essenes
They Walked with Jesus
Between Death and Life
A Soul Remembers Hiroshima
Keepers of the Garden.
The Legend of Starcrash
The Custodians
The Convoluted Universe - Book One,
  Two, Three, Four
Five Lives Remembered
The Three Waves of Volunteers and the
  New Earth
Stuart Wilson & Joanna Prentis
The Essenes - Children of the Light
Power of the Magdalene
Beyond Limitations
Atlantis and the New Consciousness
The Magdalene Version
O.T. Bonnett, M.D./Greg Satre
Reincarnation: The View from Eternity
What I Learned After Medical School
Why Healing Happens
M. Don Schorn
Elder Gods of Antiquity
Legacy of the Elder Gods
Gardens of the Elder Gods
Reincarnation...Stepping Stones of Life
Aron Abrahamsen
Holiday in Heaven
Out of the Archives – Earth Changes
Sherri Cortland
Windows of Opportunity
Raising Our Vibrations for the New Age
Michael Dennis
Morning Coffee with God
God's Many Mansions
Nikki Pattillo
Children of the Stars
A Spiritual Evolution
Rev. Grant H. Pealer
Worlds Beyond Death
A Funny Thing Happened on the Way to
  Heaven
Maiya & Geoff Gray-Cobb
Angels - The Guardians of Your Destiny
Seeds of the Soul
Sture Lönnerstrand
I Have Lived Before
Arun & Sunanda Gandhi
The Forgotten Woman
Claire Doyle Beland
Luck Doesn't Happen by Chance

James H. Kent
Past Life Memories As A Confederate
  Soldier
Dorothy Leon
Is Jehovah An E.T
Justine Alessi & M. E. McMillan
Rebirth of the Oracle
Donald L. Hicks
The Divinity Factor
Christine Ramos, RN
A Journey Into Being
Mary Letorney
Discover The Universe Within You
Debra Rayburn
Let's Get Natural With Herbs
Jodi Felice
The Enchanted Garden
Susan Mack & Natalia Krawetz
My Teachers Wear Fur Coats
Ronald Chapman
Seeing True
Rev. Keith Bender
The Despiritualized Church
Vara Humphreys
The Science of Knowledge
Karen Peebles
The Other Side of Suicide
Antoinette Lee Howard
Journey Through Fear
Julia Hanson
Awakening To Your Creation
Irene Lucas
Thirty Miracles in Thirty Days
Mandeep Khera
Why?
Robert Winterhalter
The Healing Christ
James Wawro
Ask Your Inner Voice
Tom Arbino
You Were Destined to be Together
Maureen McGill & Nola Davis
Live From the Other Side
Anita Holmes
TWIDDERS
Walter Pullen
Evolution of the Spirit
Cinnamon Crow
Teen Oracle
Chakra Zodiac Healing Oracle
Jack Churchward
Lifting the Veil on the Lost Continent of
  Mu
Guy Needler
The History of God
Beyond the Source – Book 1

For more information about any of the above titles, soon to be released titles,
or other items in our catalog, write or visit our website:
PO Box 754, Huntsville, AR 72740
www.ozarkmt.com

Other Books By Ozark Mountain Publishing, Inc.

Dee Wallace/Jarrad Hewett
The Big E
Dee Wallace
Conscious Creation
Natalie Sudman
Application of Impossible Things
Henry Michaelson
And Jesus Said – A Conversation
Victoria Pendragon
SleepMagic
Riet Okken
The Liberating Power of Emotions
Janie Wells
Payment for Passage
Dennis Wheatley/ Maria Wheatley
The Essential Dowsing Guide
Dennis Milner
Kosmos
Garnet Schulhauser
Dancing on a Stamp
Julia Cannon
Soul Speak – The Language of Your Body

For more information about any of the above titles, soon to be released titles, or other items in our catalog, write or visit our website:
PO Box 754, Huntsville, AR 72740
www.ozarkmt.com